# THE

# SOMME.

## VOLUME II.

### The Second Battle of the Somme

### (1918)

AMIENS — MONTDIDIER — COMPIÈGNE.

Compiled and published by

MICHELIN & CIE., Clermont-Ferrand, France

**Naval & Military Press**
PO Box 61
Dallington, Heathfield TN21 9ZS

The Front Line,
March 21, 1918.

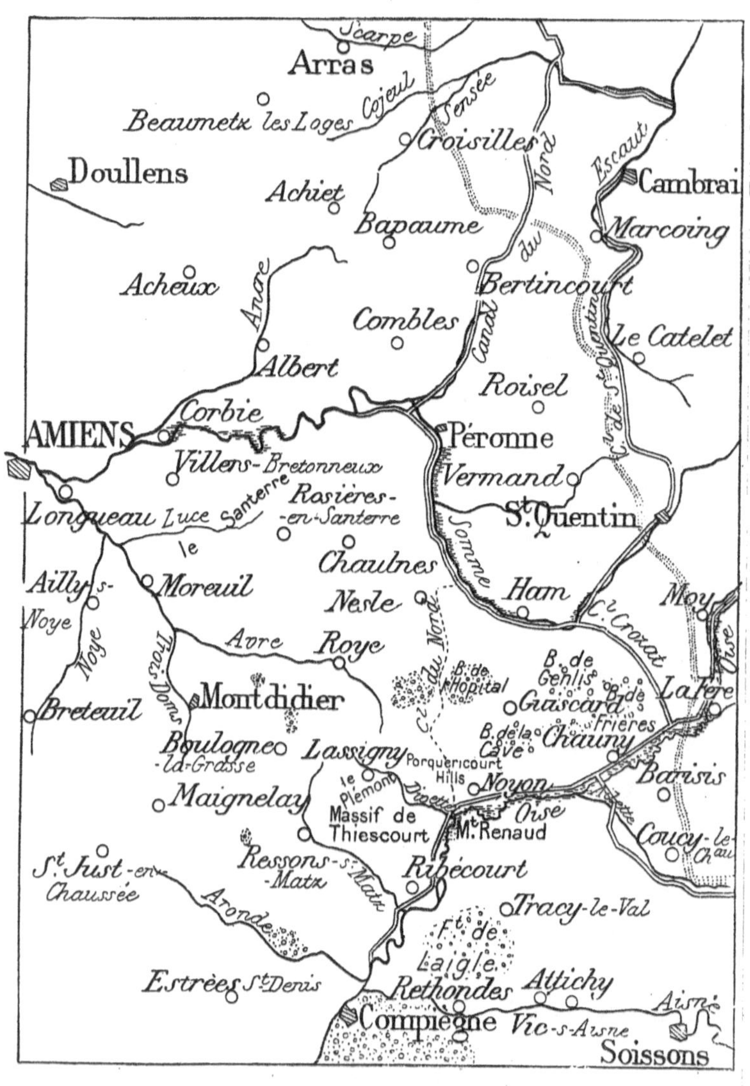


THE BATTLEFIELD.

# THE SECOND BATTLE OF THE SOMME.

At different periods during the War, important events took place in the Plains of Picardy, in the region which extends between Amiens and St. Quentin, Bapaume and Noyon, between the valleys of the rivers Ancre, Avre and Oise.

The Franco-British Offensive of July-September 1916, and the German Retreat of March 1917, are described in the Michelin Guide **" The First Battle of the Somme, 1916-1917 "**, which includes carefully prepared itineraries, enabling the reader to cover the whole battlefield of that period.

The present guide describes the operations which took place in Picardy in March-April 1918 **(The German Offensive)**, and in August 1918 **(The Franco-British Offensive)** ; in a word, the ebb and flow of the German Armies in 1918, from St. Quentin to Montdidier.

## THE BATTLEFIELD.

Driven from the banks of the Somme by the Franco-British Offensive of 1916, the Germans were compelled, in March 1917, to retreat, before the menace of the Allied offensives on their flank.

They then established themselves on the Hindenburg Line, and in 1917, in consequence of British attacks in the Arras sector and before Cambrai, they unceasingly increased the number of their fortified lines. This redoubtable position stretched to the west of the Cambrai-La Fère road, via Le Catelet and St. Quentin, utilising a series of natural obstacles, the most important of which were the Escaut, the St. Quentin Canal and the marshy valley of the Oise. (See the Michelin Guide **" The Hindenburg Line "**.)

But in the early days of 1918, having crushed Russia, Germany decided to assume the offensive, using the Hindenburg positions as a kind of spring-board, from which her mighty armies rushed forward to conquer France.

In February 1918, the British positions extended in front of the Hindenburg Line, as far as the village of Barisis, opposite the Forest of St. Gobain, to the south of the Oise. Three successive positions, widely separated from one another, had been actively strengthened. Moreover, the water-lines of the marshy valley of the Oise, the Crozat Canal, the loop in the Somme, and the North Canal, formed so many natural obstacles.

The Picardian Plain, with its broad and gentle undulations, dotted here and there with small woods, is closed, on the south, near the valley of the Oise, by the wooded hills of Genlis, Frières and La Cave, and to the west of the bend in the Oise, by the hills of Porquericourt and the wooded *massif* of Le Plémont, with its promontory, Mount Renaud, to the south of Noyon. Further west, the high ground of Boulogne-la-Grasse does not close the Plain of Santerre, which, between the slopes of Le Plémont and Montdidier, communicates freely with the Plain of Ile-de-France. The enclosed and wooded valleys of the rivers Avre, Trois-Doms and Luce intersect the table-lands of Santerre. Further north, stretches the old battlefield of 1916, — a chaotic waste of winding trenches and barbed wire entanglements.

In the Picardian Plain, beyond the bounds of the old battlefield, were numerous country villages, with their cottages grouped around the church. The long, straight roads, bordered with fine elms or fruit-trees, stretched as far as the eye could reach. This rich and prosperous region, with its vast fields of corn and beet, was completely ravaged by the War.

*Disruption of the British Front (March 21-22.).*   *Widening the Breach.*



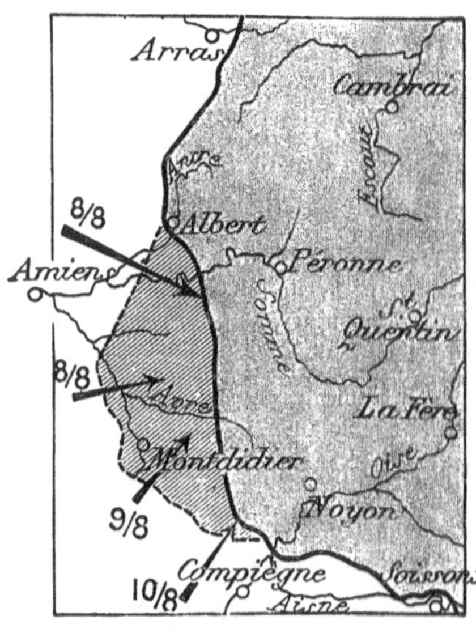


*The Offensive of August 8-12.*
*Liberation of Montdidier.*

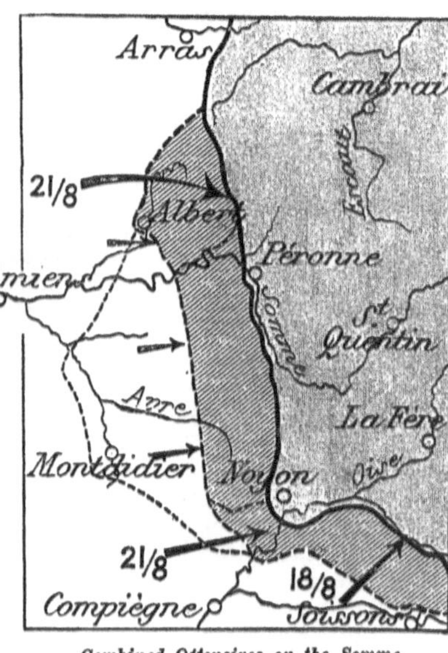


*Combined Offensives on the Somme*
*and Oise, August 18-29.*

# BATTLE OF THE SOMME (1918).

## Montdidier Pocket (March 21-April 24.)

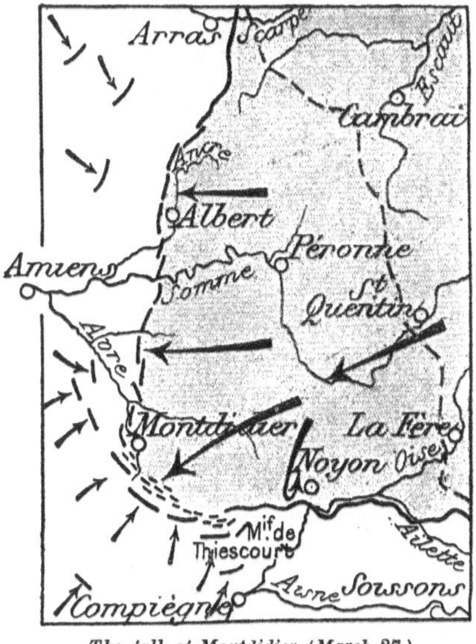


*The fall of Montdidier (March 27.).*

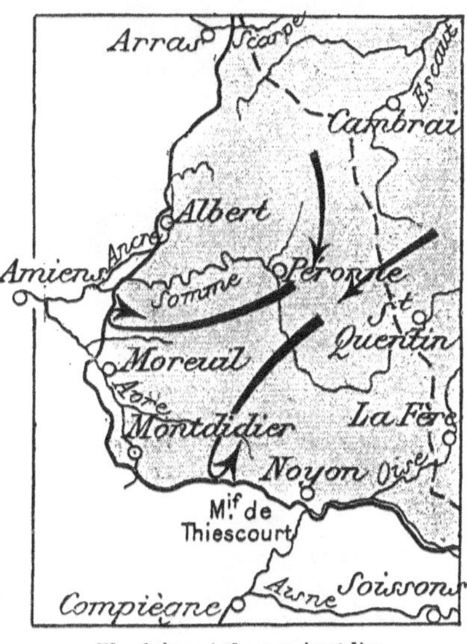


*The fixing of the new front-line.*

## the Hindenburg Line (August 8-September 25.).

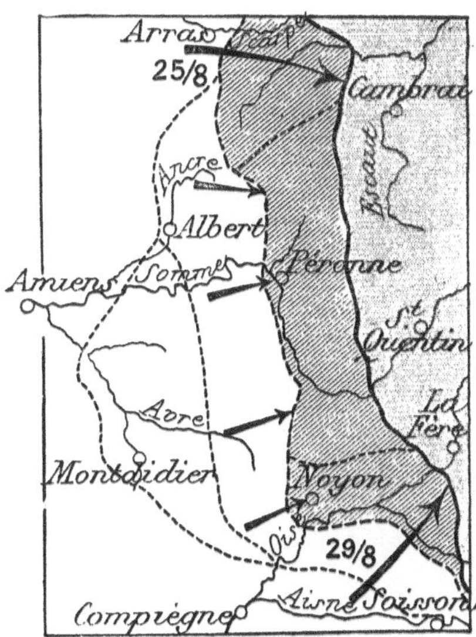


*Combined Offensives on the*
*Scarpe and Aisne, August 25-Sept. 8.*

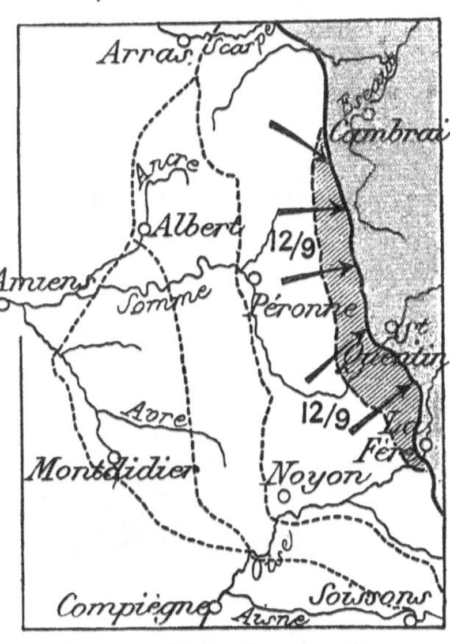


*In contact with the Hindenburg Line*
*(September 10-25).*

GENERAL PÉTAIN

FIELD-MARSHAL HAIG.

*In March 1918, the British and French Armies, under separate commands, opposed the furious attacks of numerically superior and more powerfully equipped enemy forces, grouped under the command of a single chief : Ludendorff.*

## THE GERMAN OFFENSIVE OF MARCH 21.

### The Opposing Forces — Their Material and Moral Strength.

Towards the end of 1917, the abandonment of the Allies, by Russia, was consummated by the Russo-German Armistice of December 20, followed by the Peace of Brest-Litowsk, of February 9, 1918. As early as November 1917, Germany began to transfer her legions from the eastern to the western front. Arriving, via Belgium, in ever-increasing numbers, sixty-four new divisions were thus added to her Western Armies, already one hundred and forty-one divisions strong, giving a total strength of 205 German divisions against the Allies' 177 divisions.

The material resources, accumulated on the Russian front, were likewise transferred to the western front. The enemy's artillery was reinforced all along the line, the number of heavy batteries being doubled in many of the sectors.

Besides this numerical and material superiority, Germany possessed

LUDENDORFF.

*From Genera Buat's " LUDENDORFF " (Publishers : Payot, Paris.)*

GENERAL PÉTAIN AMONG HIS " POILUS "

the additional advantage of a unique commander : Ludendorff, master of the hour, at once absolute military chief and political dictator. On the other hand, whilst the Allies were closely united by cordial friendship, sealed on the field of battle, their armies were independant units, separately commanded, each having its own reserves concentrated behind its particular front.

On February 3, 1917, the United States of America ranged themselves on the side of the Allies, but their eventually powerful effort could not make itself seriously felt before the summer of 1918. In March 1918, four American divisions were in France, and a million more men were expected by the following Autumn, but the Germans were convinced that they would have the Allies beaten before then.

The moral strength of the opposing forces constituted one of the most important factors of victory.

During 1917, after the Allies' Spring Offensives, a wave of lassitude had lowered the fighting spirit of certain units of the French Army. However, the *morale* of the French Army had fully regained its former high level, when the great German offensive of March 1918 was launched.

The British Army had in the meantime perfected its training, and acquired, in addition to experience, splendid fighting qualities.

The Germans, badly shaken in 1916 by their failure at Verdun and by the Allies' Offensive on the Somme, had, in consequence of Russia's collapse, recovered all their former arrogant confidence and pride.

But the Allies' blockade, despite Germany's ruthless submarine warfare, tightened, and each day the menace of famine increased.

Triumphal announcements of victory, and promises of an early German peace appeared periodically in their press, yet still the war dragged on. Something had to be done to end it all, whatever the cost, and so the " Peace Offensive " was decided on.

Although inferior in numbers and equipment, the Allies had acquired moral superiority.

## The German Strategy and Tactics.

In all the previous offensives, especially that of the Somme in 1916, the artillery had been used, prior to the attack, to destroy the adversary's defences. The great number of fortified works and their ever increasing strength necessitated a proportionately longer and more intense artillery preparation. Thus warned, the enemy were able to make dispositions to counteract the effects of the attack, and to bring up reinforcements.

Moreover, the tremendous pounding of the ground greatly hampered the advance of the storming troops, who were hindered at every step by the enormous shell-holes and craters.

Breaking away from past errors, and adopting and perfecting the methods inaugurated the previous year before Riga, the German High Command attacked by surprise, in March 1918, thereby securing a crushing numerical superiority. The Allies were thrown into confusion, and all attempts at resistance were unavailing, until the arrival of the reserves. During this period of complete demoralisation, the enemy were able to exploit their initial success to the full.

The method employed was that of a sudden, violent shock, preceded by a short artillery preparation, mostly with smoke and gas shells, the aim of which was to put the men out of action, rather than to crush the defences. To this end, huge concentrations of troops were effected, in such wise that the masses of men could be thrown quickly and secretly at the presumed weak part of the Allies' front.

The semi-circular disposition of the front facilitated the enemy's task, as the German reserves, grouped in the Hirson-Mézières region, in the centre of the semi-circle, could be used with the same rapidity against any part of the front-line from Flanders to Champagne.

The point chosen by Ludendorff was the junction of the Franco-British Armies. To separate these two groups, by driving back the British, on the right, and the French, on the left; to exploit the initial success in the direction of the sea, isolating the British and forcing them back upon their naval bases of Calais and Dunkirk; then, having crushed the British, to concentrate the whole of his efforts against the French, who, unsupported and demoralized, would soon be driven to their knees, — such was apparently the strategical conception of the enemy's " Kaiserschlacht " or " Emperor's Battle ".

## The Opposing Forces.

On March 21, three German armies attacked along a 54-mile front, from the Scarpe to the Oise.

In the north, the XVIIth Army (von Below) and the IInd Army (von Marwitz) attacked on either side of the Cambrai salient, but the main effort was made by the XVIIIth Army (von Hutier), which stretched from the north of St. Quentin to the Oise

Facing these armies were : the right of the British 3rd Army (B y n g), extending from the Scarpe to Gouzeaucourt, and the British 5th. Army (Gough), from Gouzeaucourt to south of the Oise.



The British expected the brunt of the attack to fall between the river Sensée and the Bapaume-Cambrai road, i. e. on the right of Byng's Army, which was reinforced accordingly, whilst the sector in front of the Oise, south of St. Quentin, against which von Hutier's huge army had been concentrated, was only held by 4 divisions.

More than 500,000 Germans were about to attack the 160,000 British under Gough and Byng, whilst from the outset of the battle, large enemy reserves swelled the number of the attacking divisions to 64, i e., more than the total number of British divisions in France. In all, no less than 1,150,000 Germans were engaged in these tremendous onslaughts.

During the five nights which preceded the attack, the German divisions had been brought up secretly, the artillery having previously taken up its positions and corrected its range, without augmenting the volume of firing, so that nothing revealed the increased number of the batteries.

The shock troops, after several weeks of intensive training, were brought up by night marches to the points of attack. During the day, they were kept out of sight in the woods or villages. At night, whether on the march or bivouacking, lights and fires were strictly forbidden. Aeroplanes hovered above the columns to see that these orders were carried out. The ammunition parks and convoys were concealed in the woods. Until the last moment, the troops and most of the officers were kept in ignorance of their destination.

These huge forces moving silently under the cover of night, symbolized the enemy's might and cunning. " *It is strange* ", wrote a German officer in his note-book, " *to think of these huge masses of troops — all Germany on the march — moving westward to-night* "

# THE BATTLE.

On March 21, during this, the " Einbruch " or piercing stage, the enormous enemy mass crushed, in less than 48 hours, the three British positions situated in front of St. Quentin. Carrying the battle into the open country beyond, the enemy transformed the " piercing " into a break-through (" Durchbruch ").

This sudden, powerful thrust was followed by a " tidal wave " of German infantry which at first submerged all before it, but which, dammed by degrees, finally spent itself, a week later, against the Allies' new front.

## THE DISRUPTION OF THE BRITISH FRONT.

On March 21, at day-break (4.40 a. m.) a violent cannonade broke out, and for five hours the intensity of this drum-fire steadily increased.

First, a deluge of shells, mostly gas, pounded the British batteries, some of which were silenced. Then the bombardment ploughed up the first positions, spreading dense clouds of gas and fumes over a wide zone.

GENERAL GOUGH.
*Photo " Daily Mirror Studios ".*

### " Michael " hour.

Under cover of the smoke and fog, the German Infantry speedily crossed No-Man's Land, and at 9.30 a. m. (" Michael" hour) penetrated the British defences.

The front assigned to each attacking division was only two kilometres wide, the troops being formed into two storm columns of one regiment each. The third regiment was kept as sector reserves, to develop initial successes.

The storm-troops, led by large numbers of non-commissioned officers, advanced in waves, shoulder-to-shoulder, preceded by a rolling barrage some 300 yards ahead of the first line. This barrage afterwards moved forward at the rate of about 200 yards every five minutes.

The waves advanced resolutely, protected first by the rolling barrage, then by the accompanying artillery and *Minenwerfer.* Wherever the resistance was too strong, a halt was made, allowing the neighbouring waves to outflank the obstacle on either side, and crush it.

GENERAL BYNG. *Photo Russell, London.*

The Germans straightway threw the greatest possible mass of infantry into the Allies' defences.

Amid clouds of gas, smoke and fog, the British in the advanced positions were surrounded and overwhelmed, often before they had realized what was happening.

Nearly all their machine-guns, posted to sweep the first zone, were put out of action.

### The First Day (March 21).

The first day of the attack, General Byng's Army from Fontaine-les-Croisilles to Demicourt, withstood the shock steadily, the Germans penetrating the first lines only.

In the centre, before St. Quentin, and to the south, in front of Moy and La Fère, General Gough's Army, overwhelmed by numbers, and notwithstanding the courage of the men, was broken early in the attack.

Opposite Le Catelet, the enemy storm divisions advanced 6 to 8 kilometres, penetrating at noon the second-line positions along the Épéhy-Le Verguier line. Further south, in front of Moy, they reached Essigny-Fargnières.

General Gough withdrew his right behind the water-line of the Crozat and Somme Canals.

### The Second Day — March 22.

Tergnier fell, and the water-line was turned from the right. Still favoured by the fog, the Germans crossed the Crozat Canal. Fresh divisions harassed the British without respite, the losses, both in men and material, being very heavy.

Their reserves, greatly outnumbered, were quickly submerged, and the third positions were lost after a desperate but ineffectual resistance.

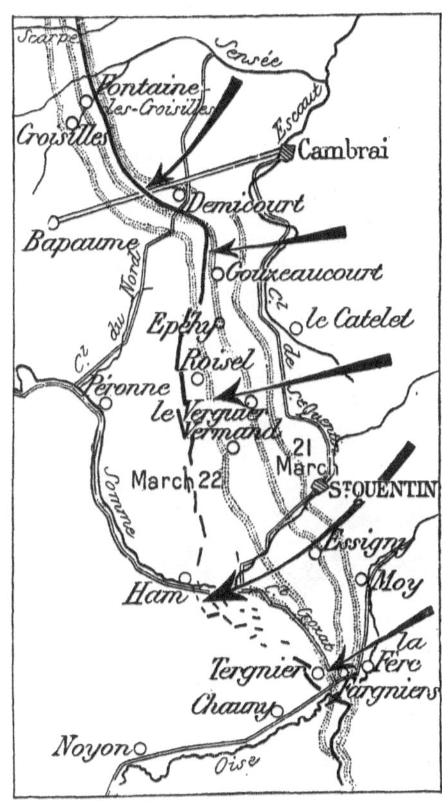


*The Disruption of the Front. March 21-22.*

In spite of its stubborn resistance, the 3rd Army (Byng) was forced to fall back, pivoting on its left, to line up with the retreating 5th Army (Gough).

The enemy advance developed rapidly. Within forty-eight hours, over 60 German divisions (750,000 men) had been thrown into the battle, which now raged in the open.

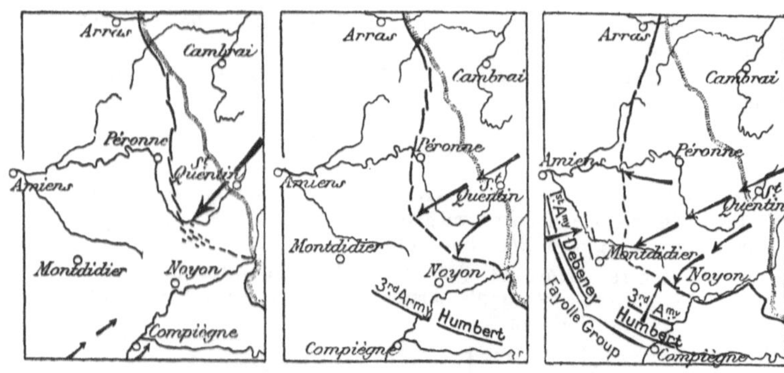

Arrival of the first French Divisions. (March 22).

Humbert's Army barring the road to Paris. (March 24).

Debeney's Army holding the enemy on the west. (March 28).

PHASES OF THE FRENCH INTERVENTION.

## THE INTERVENTION OF THE FRENCH.

The crushing of the right and centre of the British 5th Army opened a large breach north of the Oise, through which, as early as March 21, the Germans streamed south and west. The situation was critical, as the enemy hordes, having broken through the fortified zone, threatened to submerge all before them. Prompt intervention was imperative, in order to retard the enemy at all cost.

GENERAL PELLÉ REVIEWING THE TROOPS OF THE 5TH CORPS IN 1917.

As early as the evening of the 21st, General Pétain made dispositions to support the British right. The 9th and 10th Div. (5th Corps) and the 1st Div. of unmounted Cuirassiers (Pellé), in reserve near Compiègne, received orders to hold themselves in readiness. At the same time, the staff of Gen. Fayolle's Army Group, and that of Gen. Humbert's Army, prepared to take over the direction of the operations.

The 125th Inf. Div. was pushed forward to the Oise, whilst the 22nd, 62nd, and 1st. Cavalry. Divn. (Robillot's Group) were rapidly despatched to the weak points of the battle line.

This newly formed group was placed under the command of Gen. Robillot of the 2nd Cavalry Corps.

Rushed up in lorries, the first French divisions were thrown into the thick of the battle without waiting for their artillery. Heroism often made good the lack of equipment and munitions.

## THE BATTLE OF DISRUPTION.

Once the fortified zone crossed, the German armies pushed westward rapidly.

On March 23, the French Cavalry Divisions were engaged, with their armoured cars and groups of cyclists. Thanks to their great mobility, the situation was repeatedly saved. Galloping from breach to breach, the Cavalry, dismounting, stayed the enemy advance until the arrival of the infantry.

The armoured cars raided the enemy's lines unceasingly and harassed their troops with machine-gun fire. They were also used for bringing up supplies to the first-line troops and for maintaining the different liaisons. Their splendid work, with that of the Cyclist Corps, greatly helped to stay the enemy thrust.

The retreat of the British was also covered by detachments of cavalry, mounted artillery, armoured cars and tanks, which vigorously attacked the assaillants.

The Air Service likewise rendered invaluable aid.

On the evening of the 22nd, General Pétain gave orders for every available bombing plane to be used to retard te enemy advance, until reinforcements could be brought up. The air squadrons met a few hours later at the assigned point, some of them having flown ninety miles. On the way, they dropped their loads of bombs on German troops which were crossing the Somme, north of Ham, thereby retarding the advance of two enemy divisions which were preparing to outflank the British.

On the 23rd, at noon, a hundred aeroplanes, skimming just over the Germans' heads, wrought indescribable havoc and confusion in their ranks. Priceless hours were thus gained.

THE EFFECTS OF AERIAL BOMBARDMENT.

*Photographed in the Ardennes, in October 1918. A German munition train, bombed by aeroplanes, blew up, destroying the line and the artillery limbers which were being loaded. The dead horses and broken limbers are plainly visible. One may imagine the ravage caused by the Allies' aerial bombardments among the enemy concentrations in the Somme.*

## Crossing the Water-line of the
## Crozat Canal, Somme and Tortille (March 23-24).

Whilst Byng's Army withstood the enemy's onslaughts, that commanded by Gough was dislocated by the powerful thrust of von Hutier's Army.

On the **morning of the 23rd**, the remnants of the British 3rd and 18th Corps were thrown back across the Crozat Canal, among the French divisions which were taking part in the battle between the Somme and Oise, and with which they were assimilated.

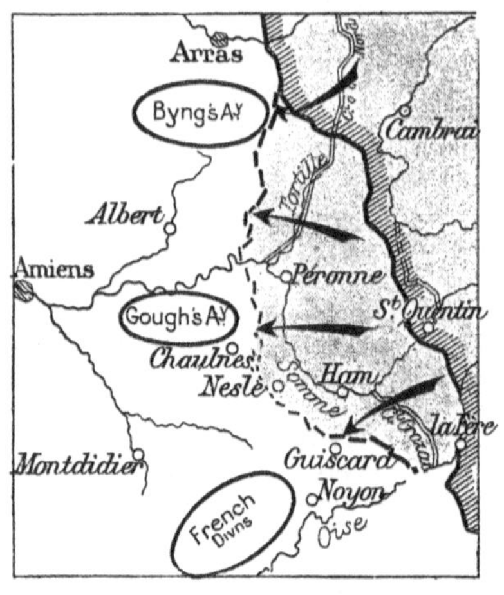


Further north, his divisions heavily depleted, and reinforcements coming up only slowly, General Gough abandoned the strong Somme-Tortille line, and continued his retreat westward, towards his reserves in the old battlefield of 1916.

The same day, the first French units to arrive were thrown between Crozat Canal and the woods of Genlis and Frières, linking up, on their right, with the 125th Division, detached from the left of the 6th Army, and established astride of the Oise, in front of Viry. (*Sketch below*).

The 1st Division of dismounted Cuirassiers (Brécart) vigorously attacked the enemy, and succeeded in staying their thrust towards the Oise. The 9th Division (Gamelin) barred the Ham-Noyon road, along a ten mile front. On their left. the 10th Division (Valdant) held the zone north of Guiscard.

*The French Divisions were engaged from the Oise to Nesle, before Noyon, which the British retreat eft unprotected.*

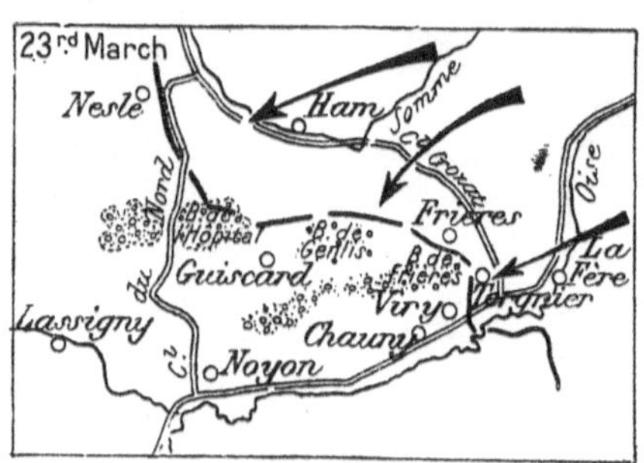


On the evening of the 23rd, the situation was critical. Genera Pellé's divisions retarded the German advance in front of the Chauny-Noyon region, which they were covering, but the enemy held Ham. In their retreat, the British constantly bore to the north-west.

The 1st Cavalry Division (Rascas), and the 22nd (Capdepont) and 62nd (Margot) Divisions arrived, and were thrown into the battle between Guiscard and Nesle, where they attempted to join hands with the

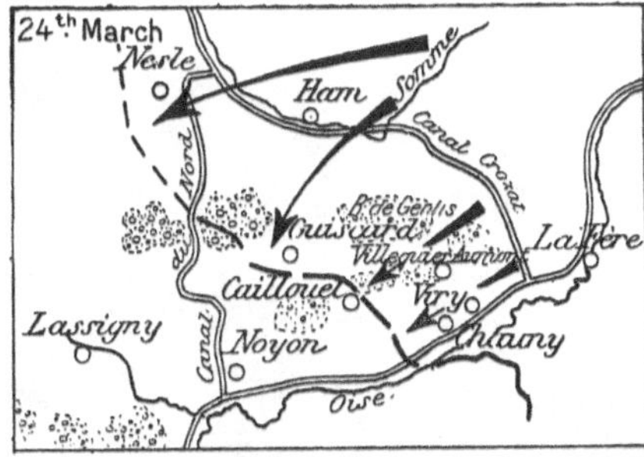


*Converging on Noyon, the Germans effected a breach north of Nesle.*

French 10th Division on their right and with the British on their left.

The same day, the German long range "Bertha" guns began to bombard Paris, in the hope of spreading panic and disorder there.

On **March 24**, the crushing effect of the German thrust was further accentuated by the arrival of new enemy divisions.

Favoured by the fog, which entirely hid the valleys of the Oise and Somme, their advance-guards swept the plain with machine-gun fire, in their search for gaps and weak places in the thin French line.

All the attacks converged towards Noyon. At 9 a. m., in the valley of the Oise, the capture of Viry-Noureuil threatened Chauny, whilst in the centre, Villequier-Aumont and Genlis Wood were taken. Overwhelmed by numbers, the Cuirassiers, after firing their last cartridges, fell back on Caillouel Hill. The divisions on the left took up positions south of Guiscard. In spite of the unequal struggle, the fighting spirit of the troops remained admirable.

On the left of General Pellé's group, between Nesle and Guiscard, the situation was still more desperate, as, having crossed the Somme, the Germans now greatly intensified their thrust. The depleted British units continued their retreat westward, leaving a gap north of Nesle. The French 22nd Div. was hurriedly despatched towards Nesle, and elements of the 1st Cav. Div. to the east of Chaulnes.

On March 24, south of Péronne, the German IInd Army crossed with difficulty the marshy valley of the Somme, then pushing on towards Chaulnes, opened a gap at Pargny.

North of Péronne, the enemy reached Sailly-Saillisel, Rancourt and Cléry in the morning, and pushed west with 3,000

GENERAL HUMBERT.

SHARPSHOOTERS AT THE SIDE OF THE ROAD.

FRANCO-BRITISH LINE OF INFANTRY IN WHICH "TOMMIES" MINGLED WITH "POILUS"
(*Photo Imperial War Museum*).

*One of the gravest consequences of the retreat of Gough's Army was the temporary severance of the French from the British. To restore and consolidate the liaison was the constant aim of the French General Staff.*

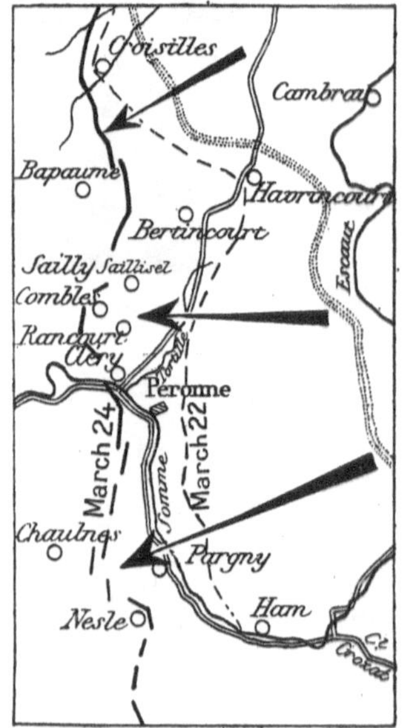


cavalry. In danger of being turned, Byng's Army, which had abandoned the Havrincourt Salient during the night of the 22nd, evacuated Bertincourt and retreated westward.

*These units coolly withdrew, whenever they found themselves outflanked and in danger of being cut off, often fighting furious rearguard actions, and repulsing the enemy with heavy loss, each time a frontal attack was attempted. (Field-Marshal Haig).*

On the contrary, we read in Ludendorff's Memoirs that *the German XVIIth Army was exhausted, having suffered too heavy losses before the Cambrai Salient on March 21 and 22.*

During the night, the enemy continued to press forward in the fog, in an attempt to rout the precariously installed and ill-supplied French units, and to harass Gough's Army, in retreat towards the Santerre Plateau. On this, Palm Sunday evening, Holy Week opened tragically.

## The Fall of Noyon and the Fighting on
## the old Battlefield of the Somme.

**The 25th, at daybreak,** fresh German divisions violently attacked the exhausted French units, seeking to turn their left wing, and at the same time crush General Pellé's group in the centre.

In face of the increasing danger, General Pellé received orders to " check the enemy advance, whatever the condition of the men might be ".

The 1st Inf. Div. (Grégoire), hastily brought up and reinforced by the remnants of the British 18th Div. and of various French Divisions picked up on the way, established itself on the hills which cover Noyon to the north-east. They had scarcely taken up their positions, when the Germans attacked, only to be repulsed. Further to the left, the enemy were unable to debouch from Crisolles, but on the French right, the 55th and 125th Div., which had been fighting incessantly since the 22nd, were forced back across the Oise, near Brétigny. Pushing on, the Germans captured Bœuf, but a British counter-attack forced them to fall back slightly.

The battle continued to rage and the danger of being outflanked became more and more acute. Catigny and Beaurains fell, leaving Noyon unprotected on the north-west. In the course of a fierce counter-attack, the 144th Inf. Reg. succeeded in recapturing these villages, but the German hordes still pressed on, opening a gap between Beaurains and Genvry, through which they poured, following the little valley of the Verse which slopes down towards Noyon. The troops defending the northern and north-eastern approaches to that town were now threatened with being surrounded.

General Pellé endeavoured to stop this fresh gap with the few units left at his disposal, and organized a new line of support on Porquericourt Hill and Mont Renaud (*sketch, p.* 18), at the same time urging the troops which were fighting to the north of Noyon to " hold out a few hours longer, each hour being worth a day".

One French division, and units of a second division, comprising some British remnants, were now fighting against odds of four to one.

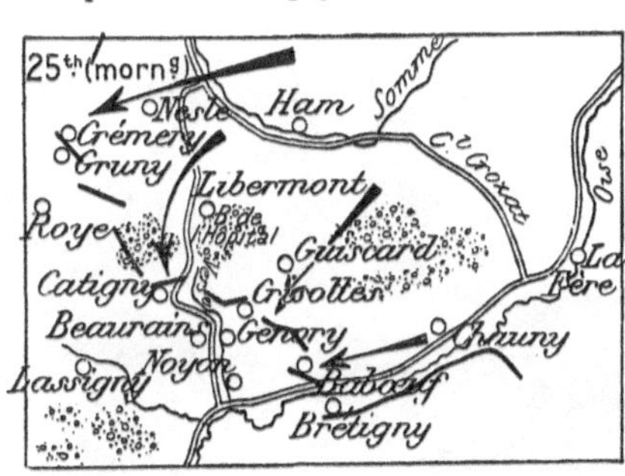


*The enemy threatened Noyon, through the valleys of the Oise and Verse. To the north of Nesle, the Montdidier road was open.*

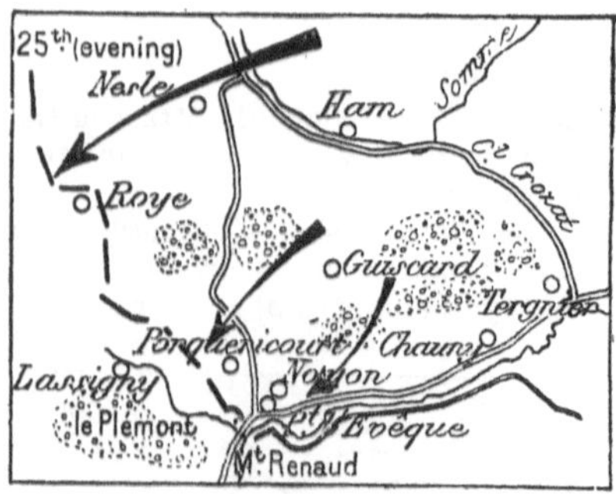

*Fall of Noyon. Gen. Pellé's Group organized positions on Porquericourt Hill and Mont-Rennud. Gen. Robillot's forces fell back on Roye.*

On the **evening of the 25th**, they fell back in good order, on Noyon. The 57th Inf. Reg. resisted all night in the town, to enable the final line of resistance to be organized.

At midnight, the front line passed in front of Porquericourt Hill and Mont Renaud, at Pont-l'Évêque, thence following the Oise. It was along this line that Gen. Pellé's Corps hadorders tohold the Germanadvance, and bar the road to Paris.

General Humbert declared on the evening of the 25th :

*The troops of the 5th A. C. and of the 2nd C. of unmounted Cavalry are defending the very heart of France. The consciousness of the grandeur of their task will point out the path of duty to them.*

This day (25th) was still more tragical on General Humbert's left. At daybreak, a violent battle broke out around Nesle, the town being abandoned at 11 a. m.

Spread over a too wide front, from Nesle to Guiscard, the troops under Gen. Robillot had orders to maintain the liaison on their right with Gen. Pellé's forces (retreating southward) and on the left with the depleted British units which were falling back to the northwest. The gap widened, and the enemy pressed through. The situation was highly critical, the road to Montdidier being now open.

Despite their desperate resistance and the untiring activity of the 1st Cav. Div. and 2nd Corps — units of which galloped from

GENERAL FAYOLLE, IN COMMAND OF THE HUMBERT-DEBENEY ARMY GROUP

breach to breach to re-establish the liaison and retard the enemy onrush — General Robillot's group fell back towards Roye.

South of the Somme, the situation was still more critical. The remains of the British 18th and 19th Corps withdrew to the line Chaulnes-Frise, which they were, however, unable to hold.

Their retreat continued to the line Proyart-Rosières. No more reserves were expected for four days. Should the Germans succeed in crushing these exhausted units the road to Amiens would be open.

About six miles behind the Proyart-Rosières front, there was an old French line, partly filled in, on the Santerre Plateau, between the Somme (at Sailly-le-Sec) and the Luce (at Demuin).

A battalion of Canadian Engineers was ordered to restore it. However, there were no troops to hold it, and as its abandonment would have imperilled Amiens, Gen. Gough decided to muster an emergency detachment of engineers,

MARCH 25.

THE ROAD TO AMIENS OPEN TO THE ENEMY.

miners, electricians, mechanics, staff personnel, pupils and instructors from the schools of the 3rd and 5th Armies, and American sappers, in all about 2,200 men. This detachment, under Maj.-Gen. Carey, was ordered to hold an eight-mile front and bar the road to Amiens.

North of the Somme, the Germans attacked from Ervillers to the river; the British left stood firm, whilst on the right, the hinge formed by Byng's Army, likewise resisted. Further south, the Germans captured Maricourt, and broke through the curtain of British troops, which lost contact with one another. The Ancre was crossed, and Byng's right, pivoting on Boyelles, fell back on the line Bucquoy, Albert, Bray-sur-Somme.

General Pétain issued a stirring appeal to the men :

*The enemy is attacking in a supreme effort to separate us from the British, and open the road to Paris. At all cost, he must be held. Stick to the ground, stand firm, reinforcements are at hand. United, you will fling yourselves on the invader. Soldiers of the Marne, Yser and Verdun, the fate of France is in your hands.*

From all parts of the front, French divisions poured in. Long lines of motor-lorries sped along all the roads converging towards Montdidier. The high spirits and fine bearing of the men reassured the anxious population, who, for several days past, had heard the guns drawing nearer, and seen the endless stream of refugees fleeing before the invader.

General Debeney arrived with his staff from Toul, to take command of the 1st Army (in formation), divisions of which arrived each day.

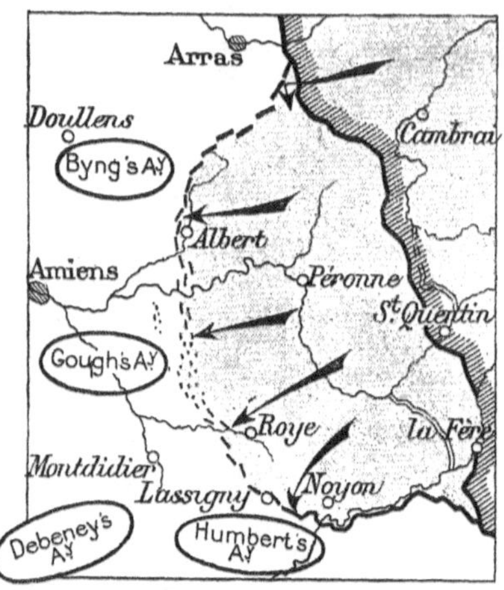


The 77th. Inf. Div. (d'Ambly) was added to the 3rd Army (Humbert). The operations of these two armies, whose task it was to bar the road to Paris and cover Amiens, were co-ordinated by Gen. Fayolle.

### The Push towards Montdidier and Fall of Roye.
### The Push towards Amiens and Fall of Albert.

On the **26th**, Gen. Pellé's group occupied Mont Renaud — a natural rampart protecting the valley of the Oise.

Determined to force a passage at all cost, the enemy attacked with fresh troops.

*The present positions must be held at all cost. The honour of each commanding officer is at stake*, proclaimed Gen. Pellé. Trenches were dug, and Mont Renaud organised. The road to Compiègne was barred and the hills to the south and south-west of Noyon became the pivot of the defences. Repeatedly attacked, Mont Renaud changed hands several times, finally resting with the French. The exhausted 10th Div. fell back on the *massif* of Le Plémont, where the 77th Div. had just taken up its positions.

However, although Gen. Humbert's right checked all enemy advance, Gen. Robillot's group and the first units of Gen. Debeney's Army, on the left, were unable to hold their ground in the Picardy Plain. Forming but a thin line, the enemy's powerful thrust opened gaps in places.

Units of the 56th and 133rd Inf. Divns. and of the 4th and 5th Cav. Divns. under Gen. de Mitry, were pushed forward, with orders to establish the liaison, on their right, with the 22nd Div., and on their left, with the British who were falling back on the Santerre Plateau. This liaison was necessarily weak, as the troops had to be deployed. Fighting day and night for every inch of ground given up, these splendid troops succeeded in retarding the enemy's advance until the arrival of reinforcements on the line of the Avre.

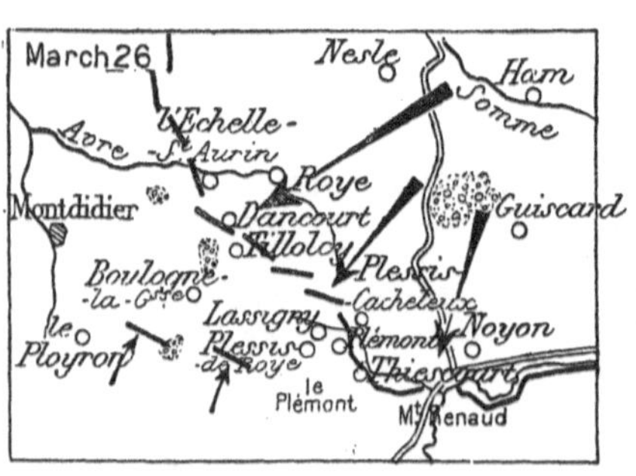


*The Germans attempted with their left to turn General Humbert's Army, strongly established at Le Plémont. Roye fell.*

The exhausted 22nd Div. fell back, carrying with it the 62nd on its right. Roye, outflanked from the south and attacked on the north, was lost. A breach, opened between the 22nd and 62nd Div. was filled by an emergency detachment hastily got together on the spot by General Robillot.

On the evening of the 26th, the front was established on the line Echelle-St.-Aurin, Dancourt, Plessis-Cacheleux.

ROYE. THE PLACE D'ARMES AT THE END OF THE WAR.

General Humbert made a strong appeal to his men : *Let all command-ing officers firmly resolve to accomplish their duty to the extreme limit of sacrifice, and imbue their men with the same spirit.*

North of the Somme, the Germans took Albert — an important junction — but were checked further north, by the left wing of Byng's Army.

THE MONT RENAUD.

## Allied Unity of Command.

Events had forcibly demonstrated the urgent necessity for Allied unity of command. On March 26, a War Council, composed of MM. Poincaré, Clemenceau, Lord Milner, Haig, Pétain and Foch, empowered the latter to *coordinate the action of the Allied Armies on the Western Front.*

" At the moment when Foch was to take precedence of Pétain and Haig, what was the position of the armies, as regards the directives of the High Command? In other words, how was the Anglo-French battle being directed? The position is defined in the General Orders of Pétain and Haig, the former of whom prescribed :

" To keep the French forces grouped, to protect the Capital; *essential mission ;*

" To ensure the liaison with the British; *secondary mission ;*

" The latter prescribed that everything possible should be done to avoid severance from the French ;

" Should this be unavoidable, *to fall back slowly, covering the Channel Ports.*

" If we place these two orders side by side, *th ir divergence strikes us painfully.* It is patent that the instructions of the two great chiefs had not the same object in view, and did not tend towards the same end. One was thinking of Paris, the other of the Channel Ports. Each would evidently consecrate tho bulk of his forces and resources to what he considered the essential task. To sum up: on the German side, there was only one battle ; *on the Allies' side, there were two : the battle for Paris, and the battle for the ports.* Had this situation continued, our defeat was certain.

BRITISH AND FRENCH REINFORCEMENTS IN A VILLAGE. (*Photo Imperial War Museum*),

" Foch's first thought, from the moment he took over the direction, was to cause this disastrous divergence to cease. To the two commanders-in-chief he prescribed the maintainance, at all cost, of the liaison between their armies. The accessory thus became the essential. The vital point was to ensure the junction between the Allied Armies, and to that end, to cover neither Paris, nor Calais, but Amiens. The battle which, till then, had been double, became single, i. e. *the Battle for Amiens.*

" Such was the strategical idea which, during the following days, Foch strove to materialise. Motoring from G. H. Q. to G. H. Q., he impressed the same thing upon all; on Haig, Pétain, Gough, the latter's successor, Rawlinson, Fayolle, Debeney and Humbert. By dint of repetition, this idea was to be deeply impressed into the minds of the executants.

" To ensure liaison, to keep the troops where they were, to prevent voluntary retreat, above all, to avoid effecting relief during the battle, to throw the divisions into the line of fire, as they arrived — such were the orders which were constantly on his lips during the days which followed ". (*La bataille de Foch*, by Raymond Recouly).

On March 28, General Pershing offered Foch the direct and immediate help of the American Forces : *I come to tell you that the American people would consider it a great honour for our troops to take part in the present battle. I ask this of you in my name and theirs. At this time, the only question is to fight. Infantry, artillery, aviation, all we have is yours.*

Henceforth, the battle was directed from Foch's head-quarters, temporarily installed at Beauvais. Twice a day, courriers maintained communications between Foch and the British and French G. H. Q's.

LINE OF BRITISH AND FRENCH SHARPSHOOTERS. (*Photo Imperial War Museum*).

## The Fall of Montdidier.
## The Growing Resistance on the Wings.

By the **27th**, the German attacks had lost much of their earlier sting. The French, whose resistance was stiffening steadily, harassed the enemy unceasingly.

Their infantry, now thirty-six miles from their base, could only be revictualled with great difficulty. The Allied airmen bombed their convoys and the railway stations incessantly.

Their artillery had difficulty in keeping up with the infantry, and the latter were not always efficiently supported.

Meanwhile, the Allies steadily organized their defences. Gen. Pellé's group, with strong positions on the bastions of the Ile de France, repulsed the enemy's repeated assaults.

Five attacks on Mont Renaud were broken.

From Canny to the Oise, the Allies stood firm.

Held on this front, the enemy deviated towards Montdidier, overwhelming Gen. Robillot's forces, which fell back on Rollot. The Germans reached Montdidier, Piennes, Rubescourt and Rollot.

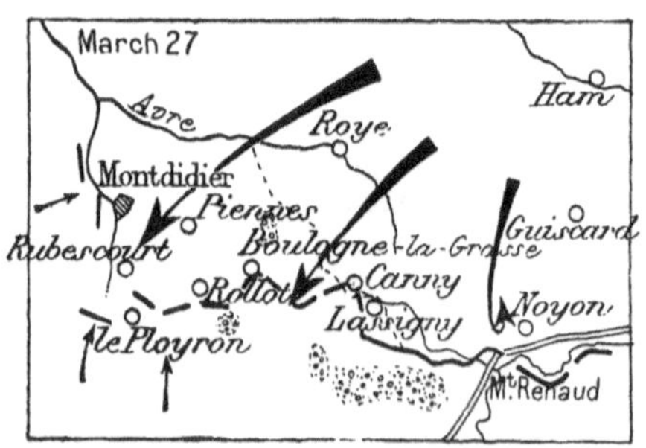


*Montdidier fell, but in face of the Allies' increasing resistance, the enemy could advance no further.*

GENERAL RAWLISON.
*Photo Russell, London.*

A few hours later, two divisions of Humbert's Army filled the breach.

Exhausted by their terrible losses, the enemy were brought to a stand.

East of Rollot, the essential portions of the massif of Boulogne-la-Grasse were strongly held.

Behind the Avre, trains and lorries were bringing up the divisions of Debeney's Army.

The British received reinforcements, and stayed their retreat in the outskirts of Albert.

The thrust against their line was now less violent, the enemy forces converging towards Montdidier.

Gen. Rawlinson replaced Gen. Gough.

A wide breach was thus made between Gen. Humbert's left and the right of Gen. Debeney's Army, then taking up its positions on the tablelands before the valley of the Avre.

It was a tragic moment. Gen. Debeney telegraphed to Gen. Fayolle : *There is a gap of nine miles between the two armies, with nobody to fill it. I ask General Fayolle to have troops brought up in motor-lorries and despatched north of Ployron, to resist at least the passing of the Cavalry.*

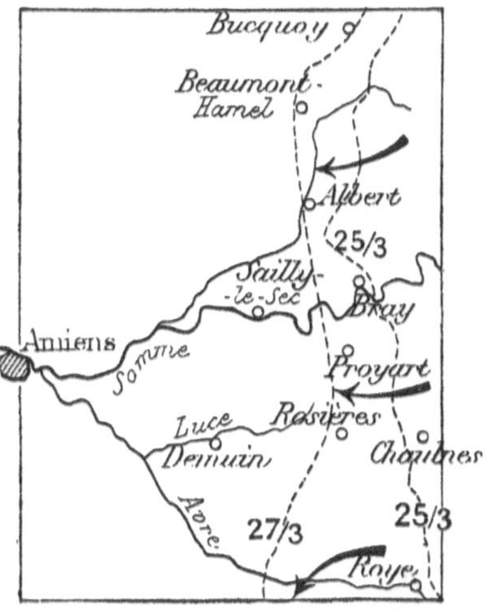


*March 26-27.*
*British reinforcements arrived north of the Somme. The Germans converged towards Montdidier.*

THE ANCRE AT ALBERT.

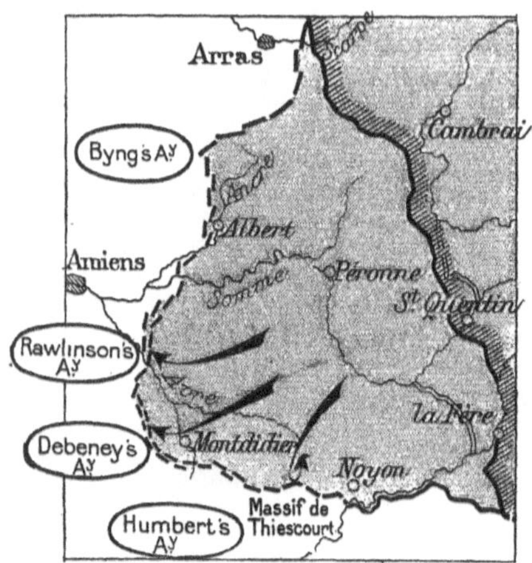



## The Battle for Amiens.
## The Allies consolidate their front and counter-attack.

After the fall of Montdidier, the fourteen divisions of von Hutier's army converged towards the pocket to the southwest.

Seven other divisions, marching against the British front between the Somme and Arras, suddenly turned south. On the 28th, 80,000 Germans made for the gap, through which 160,000 men of von Hutier's army were already pressing. In all, 240,000 men were about to attack on a seventeen-mile front.

General Humbert's left maintained an aggressive defensive. On **March 28,** they counter-attacked. The 4th Zouaves captured Orvillers and Boulogne-la-Grasse, threatening the enemy on the flank at Montdidier. Seeing the danger, the Germans retook part of the conquered positions. The moral effect was, however, considerable, indicative as it was of the Allies' determination to re-act.

On the 29th, these counter-attacks were continued, thus mobilising many

BARRICADE AT THE ENTRANCE TO MERVILLE-AU-BOIS.
(6 *kms. to the west of Moreuil*).

FRENCH ARTILLERY IN MOREUIL.

enemy units on this front, which were preparing to attack on the Avre.

During these two days, General Debeney, further north, was concentrating his forces along the front of Le Quesnel, Hangest, Pierrepont, Mesnil-Saint-Georges, Rubescourt. *There can be no question*, he declared, *of crossing to the left bank of the Avre.*

The Germans attacked at dawn on the 28th. To the west of Montdidier, Mesnil-St-Georges was captured. The 166th Division, which had just detrained, stayed the thrust at Grivesnes and Plessier. A battalion of the 5th Cav. Div. fighting on foot, recaptured Mesnil and Fontaine-sous-Montdidier.

At the junction with the British, the attack was more violent. Capturing Hangest, the Germans slipped along the valley of the Luce, driving back the British. The resistance of the latter stiffened, however, and they maintained their positions on the right bank of the Avre.

On the 29th, the enemy renewed the attack with fresh divisions, especially at Demuin and Mézières, where the defenders were driven back along the Avre. However, Gen.



*On March 29, the Germans were firmly held at the bottom of the pocket.*

Debeney's Army was now completed by the arrival of the 127th, 29th and 163rd Divisions. Its junction with the British, was strongly reinforced.

Before Arras, astride the Scarpe, the British fell back into line with Byng's Army, repulsing several violent attacks. (*Sketch, p.* 26).

On the evening of March 29, the enemy were firmly held at the bottom of the pocket, the sides of which stood firm.

## The General Attack at the bottom of the Pocket and the holding of the German Advance.

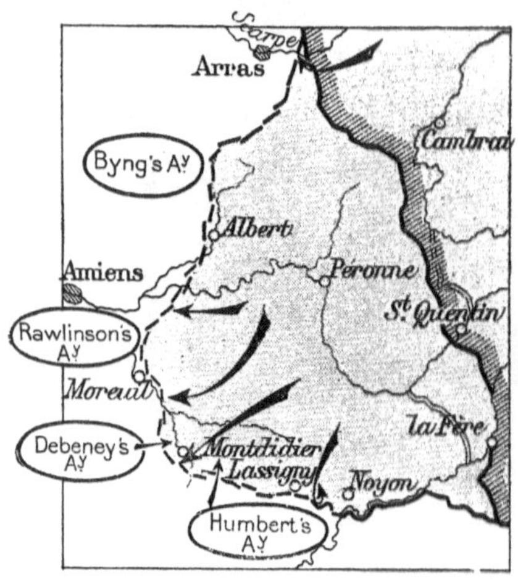


On **March 30,** the Germans launched a general attack along a thirty-mile front, from Moreuil to Noyon, against the armies of Humbert and Debeney. This was their last effort in the southward push.

In many places, the French heavy artillery had not yet taken up its new positions. The battle was therefore mainly one of infantry. To the Air Service fell the task of making good the deficiency, and throughout the battle, bombs were rained upon the railway-stations, columns of German infantry, and enemy supply convoys, whilst the fighting section, skimming over the enemy masses, riddled them with machine-gun fire.

In front of Humbert's Army, the French lines were practically intact. Homeric combats were delivered at Le Plémont, Plessis-de-Roye and before Orvillers.

In the region of Orvillers-Sorel, the 38th Div. repulsed four assaults delivered by the 4th Div. of the Prussian Guards.

The attack against the front of Debeney's Army was delivered with equal fury.

On its right, not an inch of ground was lost. All assaults on Mesnil-Saint-Georges were repulsed. The 6th Corps maintained practically all its positions intact, except before Hill 104, where a slight withdrawal was necessary.

On the left wing, the 36th Corps (Nollet) was forced to give way, and fell back on the Avre. Moreuil was lost in the evening of the 30th.

**March 31** was marked by extremely violent local actions, especially at Mesnil-St-Georges and Grivesnes, without appreciable result for either side,



THE ENEMY'S FINAL EFFORT SOUTHWARDS,
March 30-April 5.

MONTDIDIER IN GERMAN HANDS.
*The Palais de Justice (see p. 99). Across the street: A German Notice-Board.*

On the evening of the 31st, the French front, practically intact, passed west of Moreuil, skirted the high ground on the left bank of the Avre, running thence west of Cantigny, round Montdidier, along the suburbs of Orvillers, through Roye-sur-Matz, Le Plémont and the hills to the south of Noyon, where the Germans had been unable to gain a footing.

**April 1st.** The enemy sounded the French lines at Rollot, south-east of Montdidier, but were smartly checked by a vigorous counter-attack. Three attacks in front of Grivesnes were likewise repulsed.

April 2 and 3 were fairly quiet, being the prelude to the final effort against Debeney's Army.

**April 4th.** At day-break, an intense artillery preparation began, extending from the north of Hangard to the south of Grivesnes. At 7.30 a. m., the attack was launched with unheard — of violence.

Against this front, only nine miles wide, fifteen divisions — seven of which were composed of fresh troops — attacked ten times in the course of the day.

Before Grivesnes, four attacks were repulsed, whilst all the enemy's efforts against Cantigny and Hill 104 broke down. Further north the Germans captured Mailly-Raineval, Morisel and Castel.

The next day (**April 5th**), counter-attacks checked the Germans, prevented them exploiting their success north of Montdidier, and drove them back into Mailly-Raineval and Cantigny.

On the following days, fighting took place at different points, which changed hands several times, but these actions were of a local nature only.

## The Results of the German Offensive of March 21.

The great German attack was over. The roads to the south-west were barred, as those to the south, at Noyon, had been, and Gen. Debeney was able to address the following order to his troops:

*Soldiers of the 1st Army,*

*You have carried out your arduous task well.*

*Your tenacious resistance and vigorous counter-attacks have broken the onrush of the invader, and ensured the liaison with our brave Allies, the British. The great battle has begun. At this solemn hour, the whole country is with us. The soul of the Mother-land uplifts our hearts.*

On April 4, the great battle — of which the battles for Amiens, Montdidier and Compiègne were only episodes — came virtually to an end.

For ten days, after breaking the Allies' front, the Germans were able to change the war of positions into one of movement, but by a tremendous effort the French Army threw itself across their path and, as at Verdun in 1916, checkmated them.

This warfare in the open did not give the results expected by the enemy, who failed either to separate the Allies, or to rout them. On the contrary, by bringing about Allied unity of command, they strengthened the hands of their adversaries, to their own undoing.

Although the Germans captured Montdidier, they failed to reach either Amiens or Compiègne, and whereas the British, at first severely shaken, fully recovered, whilst only a portion of the French reserves were engaged, the enemy used up a considerable part of their finest troops and shock divisions, mown down in tens of thousands along the road to Paris, by the Allies' machine-guns and field artillery.

By March 31, ninety enemy divisions had been engaged, twenty-five of which had to be withdrawn on account of excessive casualties, some of them (e. g. the 45th Reserve, certain units of the 2nd Guards and 5th Infantry) having lost 50 °/o of their effective strength. The casualties of the 6th, 195th, 4th, and 119th divisions attained 75 °/o. At the very lowest estimation, the Germans lost at least 250,000 men.

The Kronprinz had promised his men that the Easter bells would ring in the long-expected peace, but Easter Sunday found the Allies more closely united than ever, awaiting with confidence the end of the battle, and determined to win through to victory.

The check of April 4 saw the end of von Hutier's reserves. All the divisions of the XVIIIth Army had been engaged, most of them with heavy casualties. Unwilling to take any of the divisions from the army group under the Bavarian Crown Prince — reserved for the proposed offensive in Flanders — or the inferior and less trained troops on the Champagne and Lorraine fronts, the German High Command, realising that the struggle must develop into one of attrition, like the first battle of the Somme, gave up for the time being all idea of an offensive on the Somme-Oise front.

A document of the German XVIIIth Army refers to the operations prior to April 6 under the name of " The Battle of Disruption " and to those which followed, under the name of " The Fighting on the Avre and in the region of Montdidier-Noyon. "

The divisions forming von Hutier's shock troops were withdrawn fairly quickly. By the end of May, only two out of the twenty-three divisions which, on March 21, had formed the XVIIIth Army, were still in line on the Moreuil-Oise front.

BRITISH BATTERIES IN ACTION IN THE OPEN. (*Photo Imperia War Museum*).

BRITISH TROOPS GOING UP THE LINE NEAR ALBERT. (*Photo Imperial War Museum*).

## The Trench Warfare Period.

From April onwards, trench warfare began again. The Allied front was reformed, consisting of a continuous line of hastily dug trenches and rapidly constructed works, held by resolute troops, whose *morale* was intact and whose fighting spirit had never been better.

Once more the heavy artillery came into requisition, for the preparatory pounding of the adversaries' positions.

In April-May, sharp engagements frequently took place at certain points. On the Luce, in the region of Hangard, on the Avre, from Thennes to Mailly-Raineval, at Grivesnes, on the west bank of the Matz, and around Orvillers-Sorel. Of these, the attack of April 24, by its violence and scope, constituted a veritable offensive against Amiens.

### The Attack of April 24
### on Villers-Bretonneux.

*See sketch opposite.*

The plateau of Villers-Bretonneux dominates the ground between the Avre and the Somme.

It was held by the British. Slightly to the south, in Hangard Woods, close to Hill 99, was the point of junction of the Allied Armies.

The enemy's main effort was made at this point, as being the weakest.

The French line started at Anchin Farm, west of Moreuil, followed the western and northern outskirts of Castel, joined up with Hill 63 on the right bank of the Avre, took in Hangard, and linked up with the British near Hill 99, to the south of Hangard Wood. From this point the British line crossed the plateau between the Avre and the Somme, between Marcelcave and Villers-Bretonneux, and passed the eastern outskirts of Hamel.

At 5 a. m., after an artillery preparation lasting an hour, the German infantry attacked.

After a desperate struggle, the enemy captured Villers-Bretonneux. Hangard fell during the night and Cachy was threatened.

The next day, a Franco-British counter-attack won back the most important part of the lost ground. Villers-Bretonneux, Hangard and Hangard Wood were recaptured and held, in spite of all the subsequent efforts of the enemy, who finally abandoned this sector in favour of Flanders.

FRENCH TRENCHES IN THE SUBURBS OF CACHY (see p. 59).

### Ludendorff's Opinion.

In his " Memoirs ", Ludendorff wrote : *The battle endea on April 4. It was a brilliant feat of arms and will always be so considered in history. What the British and French had been unable to do, we accomplished in the fourth year of the war.*

*Strategically, we did not attain what the events of March 23, 24 and 25 justified our hoping for.*

*That we failed to take Amiens, which would have rendered the communications of the enemy forces astride the Somme extremely difficult, was especially disappointing.*

*Long distance bombardment of the railways could not be considered an equivalent.*

FRENCH 6IN. BATTERY IN ACTION AT ROCQUENCOURT.
(*7 miles to the west of Montdidier*).

GERMAN HEAVY GUN AT FAVEROLLES (*2 miles east of Montdidier*).
*Captured on August 9, 1918, during the offensive of General Debeney's Army.* (See p. 42).

CLEMENCEAU AT THE G. H. Q. OF A BRITISH DIVISION IN 1918.
*(Photo Imperial War Museum).*

A GERMAN TANK TRAP. *Australian and American soldiers examine the charges of explosive with which this trap was fitted. One of them is looking through a German periscope. (July 11, 1918).*

# THE ALLIES' OFFENSIVES IN PICARDY.
### August-September 1918.

### After the German Offensive of March.

After the check of their offensive in Picardy, the Germans attempted, by means of secondary offensives, to attain those results which they had failed to obtain in the first instance.

On April 9, they attacked in Flanders, from Béthune to the north of Ypres, in the direction of the Channel Ports, but failed to take Ypres, or to reach Hazebrouck. (*See the Guide :* **Ypres.**)

On May 27, the front of the Chemin des Dames was attacked by surprise, the enemy reaching the banks of the Marne. (*See the Guide :* **The Second Battle of the Marne.**

From June 9 to 18, their efforts were turned against the salients of the Aisne and Rheims. On June 11, they captured the *massif* of Thiescourt, but were held before Compiègne. In front of Rheims the road was barred by the French Colonial troops. (*See the Guide :* **Rheims).**

Lastly, seeking a prompt decision at all cost, and hypnotised by Paris, the Germans planned a still more formidable offensive : the " Friedensturm " or Peace Battle. However, the French High Command were not taken unawares. The scope and time of the offensive were known, and the Germans failed.

### The Strategy and Tactics of the Allies.

The hour of the counter-offensive was about to strike. The Allies had overcome the crisis due to the shortage of men. The British Army had been reorganized. The American forces had greatly increased in numbers. The fighting spirit of the French was higher than ever. The material strength of the Allies was satisfactory, and included large numbers of the new offensive arm : the tank, destined to relieve and support the infantry, and combat the German shock troops.

Lastly, the Allies were now grouped under a single chief: Foch, who knew where and when to strike.

*The Allied Armies, he declared, have arrived at the turning of the ways ; in the thick of battle they have regained the initiative, and their strength enables them to retain it ; the principles of war command them to do so. The time has come to abandon the defensive attitude necessitated till now by numerical inferiority, and to take the offensive.*

*The action of the Commander-in-chief of the Allied Armies will, in future, aim at maintaining his hold on the German Commandment, giving him no respite which would allow him to recover and reconstitute his forces. To that end, separate surprise attacks will be made successively, as rapidly as possible, so as to augment progressively the disorganization of the enemy's armies and the confusion of the German Commandment, until the day of the general offensive, and of the final attack which will crumble up the whole of the adversary's front.*

A comparison of this conception of Foch's with that of Ludendorff brings out all its suppleness and power.

The counter-offensive by the armies of Mangin and Degoutte in the Château-Thierry pocket, begun on July 18, was scarcely over, when the Second Battle of the Somme broke out.

THE ALLIED MILITARY CHIEFS.
*From left to right :* PÉTAIN, HAIG, FOCH *and* PERSHING.

In this new battle of the Somme, the retreat of the German armies on the Hindenburg Line, in August-September 1918, was effected under the pressure of four successive thrusts :

I. — The operations carried out simultaneously by the British 4th Army and the French 1st and 3rd Armies against the Albert, Montdidier, Lassigny salient, to clear the Paris-Amiens railway. (*Pages* 38-45.)

II. — The British offensive north of the Somme, coinciding with the French offensive between the Oise and the Aisne. (*Pages* 46-49.)

III. — The British offensive on the Scarpe and the French offensive on the Ailette. (*Page* 50.)

IV. — The Franco-British offensive against the advanced defences of the Hindenburg line. (*Page* 51.)

# I. — THE ATTACK ON THE SALIENT OF ALBERT-MONTDIDIER-LASSIGNY.
## August 8-13, 1918.
### Preliminary Operations of July.

Throughout July, the Allies carried out different local operations, in order to improve their positions and prepare for the coming offensive.

As early as July 4, Australians supported by Americans, had begun to advance between Villers-Bretonneux and the Somme, by capturing the village and wood of Hamel.

On July 9, after a brilliant attack between Castel and the north of Mailly-Raineval, the French captured Castel, and on the 23rd, Mailly-Raineval, which brought them nearer the Avre.

These different actions, and the flattening of the Cantigny salient by the American 1st Div. on May 28, had warned the enemy.

On August 2, the Germans fell back on the Ancre, and on the 3rd to the Avre. The bulk of their forces were withdrawn east of these rivers, leaving only light forces on the west bank.

On the Marne, Ludendorff had just suffered a severe defeat. From July 18 to August 4, his armies had been driven back from the Marne to the Vesle, where they organized new positions. (*See the Guide :* **The Second Battle of the Marne.**) In the belief that this effort had temporarily exhausted the Allies, Ludendorff was planning new operations in Flanders, when he was surprised by a new and powerful Allied Offensive. From that point, the initiative remained with Foch.

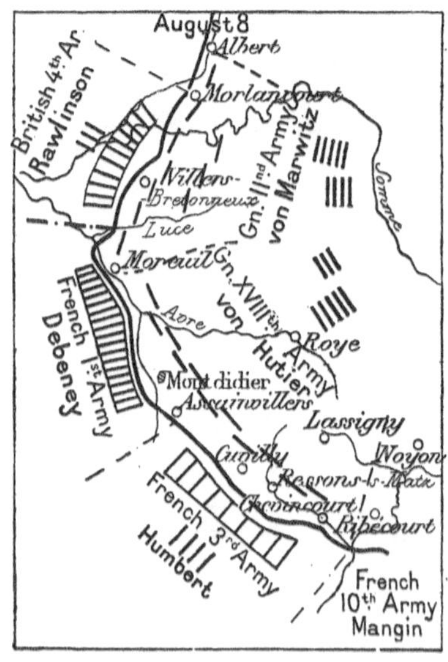


*The Front Line on August 8, and the Opposing Forces.*

### The Front Line and the Opposing Forces.

On August 8, the front line passed west of Albert, east of Villers-Bretonneux, then followed the left bank of the Avre, and the Doms stream, west of Montdidier, running thence towards the Matz and the Oise, via Assainvillers, west of Cuvilly and Chevincourt.

From north to south, the enemy front was held by the IInd Army (von Marwitz) (10 Divns. in line from Albert to Moreuil), and by the XVIIIth Army (von Hutier) (11 Divns. from Moreuil to the Oise).

These two armies, with 21 divisions in line, engaged 17 other divisions during the course of the battle, i. e. 38 divisions in all.

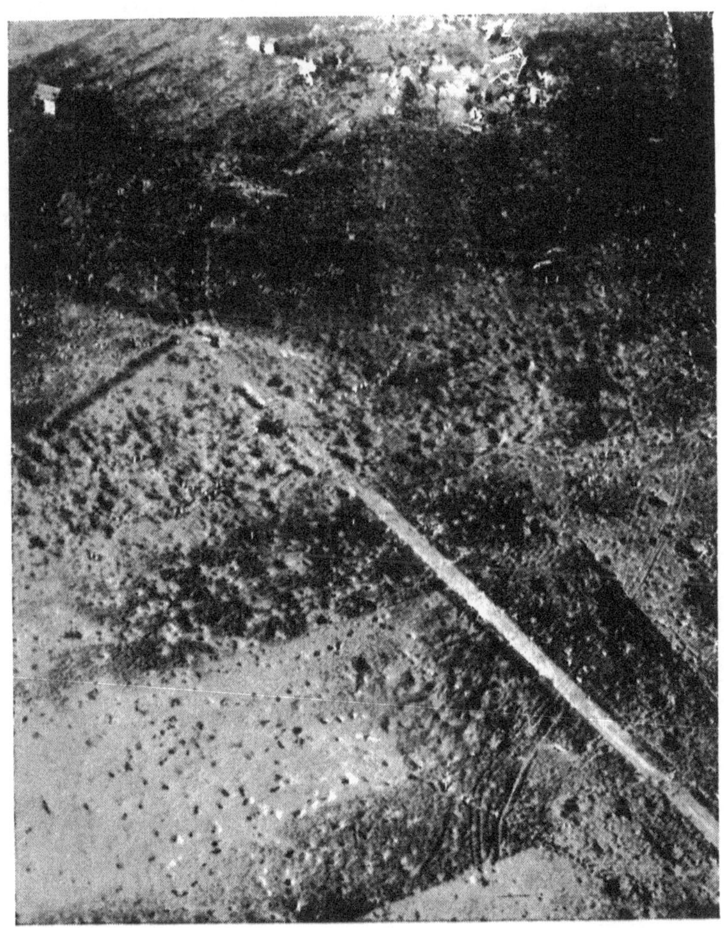

THE AMERICANS ATTACKING CANTIGNY (MAY 28, 1918).

*Photographed from an accompanying aeroplane. At the top of photo : Cantigny village. At bottom of photo : Tank tracks. The white dots and dashes spread over the photo are the American Infantry. Two larger dashes about three-quarters of an inch below Cantigny, on the right, are tanks.*

The undermentioned forces were grouped under the command of Field-Marshal Haig :

The British 4th Army (Rawlinson), comprising the 3rd Corps (3 divisions), the Australian Corps (4 divisions), the Canadian Corps (4 divisions), and 3 divisions of British Cavalry, 2 brigades of armoured cars and 1 battalion of Canadian Cyclists in reserve.

The French 1st Army (Debeney), comprising the 31st Corps (4 divisions), 9th Corps (2 divisions), 10th Corps (3 divisions), 35th Corps (4 divisions), and the 2nd Cavalry Corps in reserve.

### The Franco-British Attack of August 8, 1918.

These armies attacked on August 8, along a 15-mile front, from the Ancre to the Avre.

" *At 4. 20 a. m., after three formidable cannon-shots, —the signal for the opening of the attack,— the rolling barrage broke out before the Australian and Canadian troops, who immediately dashed forward. At the same time, the heavy and light tanks, armoured cars and motor-lorries, loaded with supplies and ammuniton, set out. At certain points, the cavalry, followed by the artillery and the aeroplanes, guarded or speeded up the advance. The enemy were taken completely by surprise. The troops and staffs were taken prisoners before they realized what had happened. One after another, the villages were surrounded and captured. Forging ahead of the infantry, the cavalry and tanks spread panic everywhere.* "

The British advanced rapidly in the direction of Rosières, along both sides of the Amiens-Chaulnes railway.

Towards evening, the advanced line passed through Mézières, Caix and Cerisy. Everywhere, except at Morlancourt, north of the Somme, where the enemy resisted desperately, the Germans were routed.

More than 13,000 prisoners, a general and the staff of an army corps, and 300 guns had fallen into the hands of the British by 9 a. m.

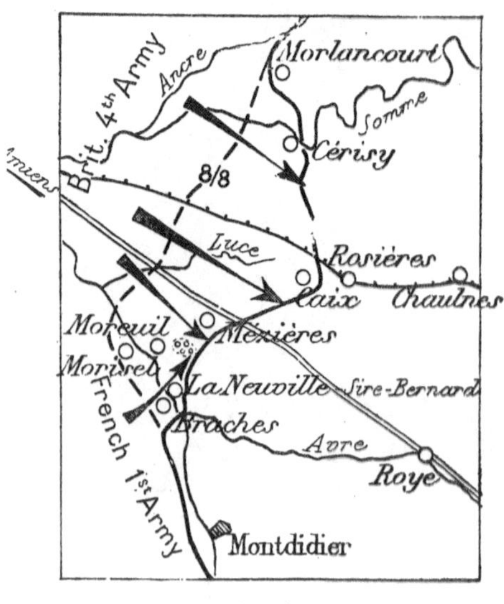


*August 8.*

Along the front of Debeney's Army, the artillery preparation was short but violent, (45 minutes). The infantry attacked about five o'clock i.e. after the British. The ground, divided for the greater part by the valley of the Avre, was more difficult, and General Debeney counted rather on maœuvering, than on surprise.

The attack began on a front of $2\frac{1}{2}$ miles, south of the Amiens-Roye road, debouching from the valley of the Luce towards ground suitable for the tanks, the troops being gradually engaged on their right, along the Avre.

At 8 a. m., two divisions turned Moreuil Wood, from the north-east and south-west. On the Avre, another division captured Morisel, whilst to the south of Moreuil a battalion crossed the river. Moreuil, turned from the north and south, fell. South of Moreuil, two fresh divisions crossed the Avre, opposite Braches, opening up a way for the troops who had to fight on the plateaux.

At the end of the day, after an advance of about five miles, the French reached the line Braches, La Neuville-Sire-Bernard, and joined hands with the British near Mézières. 3,300 prisoners, including three regimental commandants, were taken.

GERMAN ATTERY CAPTURED BY THE BRITISH, WHO IMMEDIATELY TURNED IT ON THE ENEMY.
*The third gun is still pointing towards the Allies' lines. (Photo Imp. War Museum).*

*" It was a black day for the German Army ", wrote Ludendorff, " the blackest of all the war, except September 15, which saw the defection of Bulgaria, and sealed the destinies of the Quadruple Alliance ".*

GERMAN ARTILLERY POSITION IN SUNKEN ROAD. *(Photo Imp. War Museum).*

### From August 9 to 12.

On **August 9-10**, the British thrust and the French manœuvre developed.

#### THE BRITISH ADVANCE.

Between Albert and the Amiens-Roye road, the Canadians and Australians harassed the enemy without respite, and advanced several kilometres, capturing Bouchoir, Méharicourt, Rosières, Lihons and Proyart.

North of the Somme, in co-operation with American troops, they captured Morlancourt village and plateau to the south-east, where the enemy resisted desperately.

*The Allies Advance from the morning of August 8 (dash line) to the evening of the same day (dot-and-dash line). The thick full line shows the front on August 12.*

On the **11th,** in spite of stubborn resistance, the British reached the Dernancourt crossroads, about a mile west of Bray, Chilly, Fouquescourt and the western suburbs of Villers-les-Roye.

On the **12th,** they drove the enemy for good out of Proyart. On the **13th,** they reached the suburbs of Bray-sur-Somme and the cross-roads of Chuignolles. The front now ran along the old German lines of the Somme Battlefield of 1916, where the enemy, thanks to a number of strong points of support, succeeded in staying the advance. In five days, the British had scored a fine victory, their forces (13 infantry divisions, one regiment of the American 33rd Division, 3 divisions of cavalry, and 400 tanks) defeating 20 German divisions, advancing 12 miles, and capturing 22,000 prisoners and 400 guns.

### The French Manœuvre. Liberating Montdidier.

Meanwhile, General Debeney, by a series of turning movements, brought about the fall of important sections of the German front. without frontal attacks.

Constantly extending his attacks along the Avre, the approaches to the river on the north and north-east, as far as the confluence with the Doms stream, were cleared, whilst his hold on Montdidier, from the north-east, gradually tightened.

BRITISH CAVALRY NEAR ALBERT. (*Photo Imperial War Museum*).

On **August 9,** the French line was advanced as far as the station of Hangest-en-Santerre, on the Albert-Rosières-Montdidier railway.

In order to force the enemy to abandon Montdidier, without a frontal attack, General Debeney began a turning movement at about 4 p. m. A secondary attack was launched in the direction of Roye, between Domelieu and Le Ployron. The station of Montdidier and Faverolles Village on the Montdidier-Roye line, were reached that evening.

Throughout the day, the French airmen bombed Roye undisturbed by the enemy's planes or air-defence guns.

By **evening,** the 1st Army had taken 5,000 prisoners. From Faverolles, they threatened to join up with the men who had advanced north, via Davenescourt, and to cut off the Germans in Montdidier.

The latter was evacuated in great disorder the same night and on the following morning, only a few machine-gunners being left behind to retard the French advance as long as possible.

On **August 10,** at noon, the French entered the ruined town, and advanced rapidly eastward, beyond Fescamps, on both sides of the road to Roye. In the evening, they reached the line Villers-les-Roye (where they joined hands with the British) and Grivillers.

On the **11th,** they captured the park and village of Tilloloy. By the evening of the **12th,** the 1st Army had taken 8,500 prisoners (including 181 officers), 250 guns, numerous minenwerfer, 1,600 machines-guns, and huge quantities of stores.

PHOTOS, *p.* 44:

(1) *Australian Sergeant examining a German Machine-gun captured by the 15th Brigade* (2) *Near Warfusée-Abancourt, August 8. Infantry of the Australian 1st Division advancing on Harbonnières, after a tank had cleaned up a line of German Machine-guns which was holding them* (3) *The Shelters of the above line of machine-guns-light constructions compared with the powerful trench organisations, yet strong enough to require tank treatment.*

PHOTOS ABOVE:

(1) *Australians in German trench, with field-guns just captured (August* 1918). (2) *British lorries in Villers-Bretonneux (August* 17, 1918).

## II. — THE BRITISH OFFENSIVE NORTH OF THE SOMME AND THE FRENCH OFFENSIVE BETWEEN THE OISE AND AISNE.

### August 18-29.

The first phase of the Battle of Picardy was ended, but a great new effort, between the Somme and the Scarpe, was being prepared.

Between the Aisne and the Oise, Mangin's Army attacked the plateaux on August 18th, advancing to the Ailette on the 23rd. (*Sketch opposite*).

Following up this advance, Humbert's Army continued its offensive vigorously on the 21st, conquered the northern slopes of Le Plémont, crossed the Divette, and occupied Lassigny. (*Sketch opposite*).

By their advance, these two armies threatened the right of the German XVIIIth Army, established on the Chaulnes-Roye line.

At the same time, Byng's Army attacked between the Ancre and Croisilles, whilst Rawlinson's left attacked north of the Somme. (*Sketch opposite*).

*The Attack between the Oise and Aisne by the Armies of Generals Mangin and Humbert, August 18-23.*

At dawn, on **August 21,** the 4th and 6th Corps of Byng's Army attacked between Miraumont and Moyenneville.

Supported by tanks, they captured the advance defences in brilliant style.

The fighting was particularly severe around Achiet-le-Grand and Logeast Wood, where, however, the advance continued steadily. The Arras-Albert railway which was the enemy's principal line of defence, was reached, 2,000 prisoners being taken.

After this preparatory attack, the offensive was launched on **August 22,** along a thirty-two mile front, between Lihons and Mercatel.

South of the Somme, the Australians captured Herleville and Chuignes, with 2,000 prisoners. Rawlinson's left crossed the Ancre, took Albert, and advanced its front to the hills east of the Albert-Braye road, capturing 2,400 prisoners.

But the hardest blow was struck further north by Byng's Army. Advancing beyond the principal line of defence (the Arras-Albert railway),

*The Attack between the Somme and Scarpe by Byng and Rawlinson, August 21-29*

the 4th and 6th Corps took Gomiécourt, Ervillers, Boyelles, many guns, and more than 5,000 prisoners, then pushed on towards Bapaume and Croisilles. The 6th Corps, astride the Arras-Bapaume road, marched on Bapaume, threatening to cut off the Germans who were hanging on to the Heights of Thiepval. The latter, attacked at the same time further south, fell. Bray-sur-Somme was also captured.

The battle continued from the 25th to the 29th, the enemy's resistance stiffening steadily.

Counter-attacking, the Germans defended this old battlefield of 1916, strewn with obstacles, with great desperation.

On the **29th,** Bapaume fell, and the Germans retreated from the north of that town to the Somme, on the line Cléry, Combles, Frémicourt, Bullecourt, and Heudecourt.

Threatened by the British to the north of the Somme, and by the French on the banks of the Oise, the Germans began their retreat in the bend of the Somme. Closely pursued by the British 4th Army and the French 1st and 3rd Armies, they withdrew to the river, from Péronne to Ham.

*The German Retreat, south of the Somme, under the double menace of the British and French Advance.*

Chaulnes and Nesle were occupied by the Allies.

*" On the same ground which had seen their stubborn defence, the British troops went up to the attack with untiring vigour and unshakeable determination, which neither the difficulty of the ground, nor the obstinate resistance of the enemy could break or diminish ".* (Haig).

GERMAN LONG-RANGE GUN CAPTURED BY THE AUSTRALIANS AT PROYART.

Photo Imperial War Museum.

PHOTOS, p. 48 :
(1) *The 2nd German line near Albert, occupied by the British.* (2) *The Railway Station at Albert, a few minutes after the German retreat.* (3) *Railway destroyed by the British artillery, during the advance on Bapaume.*

PHOTO ABOVE:
*Albert, seen from the interior of the Church, the day the town was liberated (Photo Imp. War Museum).*

## III. — THE OFFENSIVES ON THE SCARPE AND AILETTE.

### August 25-September 8, 1918.

Pursuing his plan of offensive, Foch extended the field of operations. Writing to Field-Marshal Haig, he said: *Continue your operations, leaving the enemy no respite, and developing the scope of your actions. It is this increasing breadth of the offensive, fed from the rear and strongly pressed in front, without limitation of objective, without consideration for the alignment and too close liaison, which will give us the greatest results with the least losses... The armies of General Pétain are going forward again in the same manner.*

At the time Mangin's Army was preparing to crush the enemy's front between the Aisne and St. Gobain, Horne's Army, on the Scarpe, attacked the salient east of Arras.

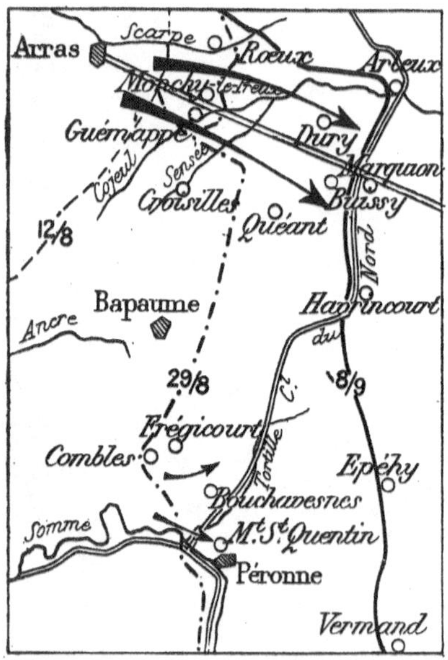


On **August 25,** the Canadians, astride the Scarpe, and the left of Byng's Army captured the difficult positions of Monchy-le-Preux, Guémappe and Rœux, bringing their line into contact with the redoubtable position of Quéant-Drocourt, a ramification of the Hindenburg Line.

On **September 2,** the Canadians attacked, progressing rapidly along the Arras-Cambrai road. Penetrating the German lines to a depth of 6 miles, they reached Buissy.

On the night of August 30, the Australians, in the centre, furiously attacked and captured the formidable bastion of Mont-St-Quentin. On **September 1,** they entered Péronne, after desperate fighting. To flank this attack on the north, Bouchavesnes and Frégicourt were captured.

Further south, on the Oise, Humbert's Army, in spite of the enemy's resistance, took Noyon and the high ground dominating the town. Advancing from the Ailette, towards Chauny, Mangin's left reached the outskirts of St. Gobain Forest, in the old lines of March 1918.

Outflanked on the north, towards Cambrai, and on the south along

the Oise, in the direction of La Fère, and violently attacked at the same time in the centre at Péronne, the Germans retreated towards the Hindenburg positions. The British and French forces drove back the enemy rear-guards, which were unable to hold the line of the Tortille and the Canal du Nord.

On **Sept. 8,** the Allied front ran west of Arleux and **Marquion,** through Havrincourt, Épéhy and Vermand, then followed the Crozat Canal.

## IV. — THE OFFENSIVES AGAINST THE OUTWORKS OF THE HINDENBURG LINE.
### September 10-25.

The Germans had reached the advanced defences of their famous Hindenburg Line, consisting of the old British lines lost in March. These formidable positions protected the ramparts of the Hindenburg Line, said to be impregnable.

On **September 10,** the British 3rd and 4th Armies (Byng and Rawlinson) attacked between Havrincourt and Holnon.

The 4th Army took Vermand, the western outskirts of Holnon Woods, and gained a footing in Épéhy and Jeancourt. On the **13th,** after desperate fighting, it captured the woods and village of Holnon.

The 3rd Army crossed the Canal du Nord, south of the Bapaume-Cambrai road, turned the positions from Havrincourt to Gouzeaucourt, and captured the greater part of them, the enemy resisting desperately.

The same day (Sept. 12), the American 1st Army captured the whole of the St. Mihiel Salient, with 15,000 prisoners and 200 guns. (*See the Guide :* **The Battle of St. Mihiel.**)

On the **18th,** a general attack was launched by the British 3rd and 4th Armies, in liaison with the French 1st Army. All the enemy's positions between Gouzeaucourt and Holnon were captured, with 10,000 prisoners and 150 guns.

To the south, Debeney's Army took over the front of Humbert's Army — transferred to the sector of the 10th Army — the latter, due to the shortening of the front, being sent to Lorraine, for a new offensive.

Debeney's Army, extending south of the Oise, attacked, and after capturing Dallon Spur, Castres and Essigny-le-Grand, reached the valley of the Oise, from Vendeuil to La Fère.

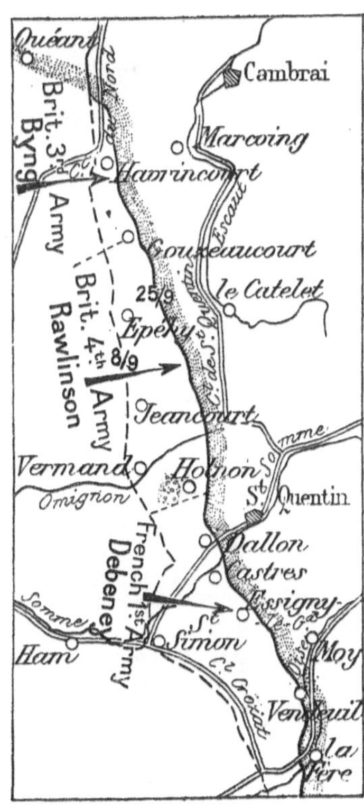

PEACE AFTER STRIFE. LIFE IN THE RUINS.
*Méharicourt, between Chaulnes and Caix, in 1919*

Disorganized and exhausted, their ranks depleted, the enemy were now incapable of attempting a counter-offensive.

To avoid this continuous, exhaustive battle, the Germans sought refuge in positions which they believed to be impregnable, and where they hoped to rest, reorganize and reconstitute their reserves.

This was an imperious necessity, as from July 15 to September 25, 163 of their divisions had been engaged, 75 of them two or three times.

On September 26, despite a reduction of 120 miles in the length of the front, they were forced to maintain practically the same number of divisions in line as on July 15, owing to their decreased effective strength and fighting value.

Moreover, to keep these forces effective, ten divisions had to be dissolved, and the battalions of fifty others reduced from four to three companies. Large numbers of men were called up from the works, in order to husband their last resources — the 1920 recruits.

Everywhere, the Allied armies were in contact with the Hindenburg Line, ready for the grand assault against the formidable positions from which the enemy had set out on March 21 for Paris and victory.

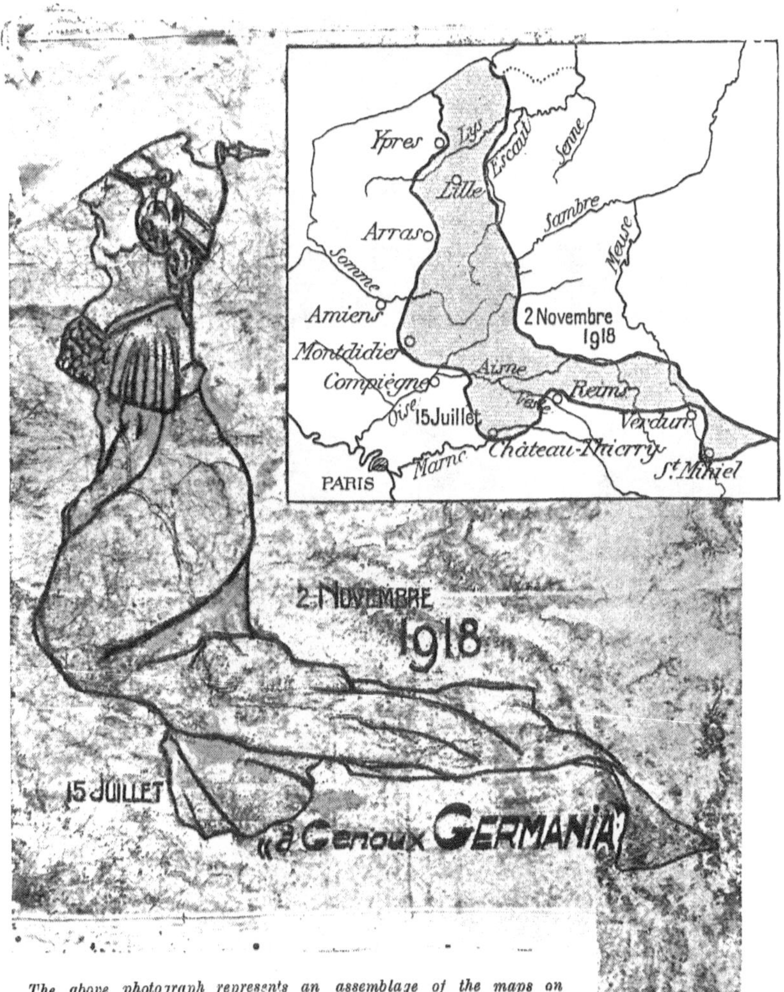



*The above photograph represents an assemblage of the maps on which the Staff of the French 20th Corps traced the front from day to day.*

*By bringing out the two lines of July 15 and November 2 (exactly reproduced), and by adding a few unimportant touches inside and the spike of the helmet, one of the Staff draughtsmen obtained this curious figure of Germania on her knees.*

*With the help of the inset sketch-map, it is easy to trace the salients of Ypres, Arras Montdidier, Château-Thierry (crossed by the Vesle), Rheims, Verdun, and St. Mihiel.*

In six weeks, by repeated, inter-related attacks, vigorously executed without respite, the Allies had flattened out the salient from St. Quentin to beyond Montdidier and Albert, produced by the German push.

The end was near. To avoid a military disaster without precedent in the world's history, the enemy soon afterwards sued for an armistice and peace.

*Ginchy (between Bapaume and Péronne) bombarded by the British (July 11, 1916).*

*Ginchy, ten days later (July 21, 1916).*

*Ginchy, two days before its capture by the British (Sept. 7, 1916).*
ILLUSTRATING THE PROGRESSIVE DESTRUCTION OF A VILLAGE BY ARTILLERY.
*Taken from the Michelin Guide:* " THE FIRST BATTLE OF THE SOMME ".

MODERN WAR WEAPONS.

*A heavy trench-mortar of the 3rd Australian Medium Trench-Mortar Battery in action at Ville-sur-Ancre, on May 29, 1918, when the German front line was only 400 yards beyond this farm-house.*

PÉRONNE IN 1918. THE GRANDE PLACE. CAPTURED GERMAN GUNS.

*Taken from the Guide :* THE FIRST BATTLE OF THE SOMME.

AMIENS, DURING THE GERMAN OFFENSIVES OF 1918.
(1) *Fire at the Saint-Frères Works, April 23, 1918.*
(2) *Platforms at the Gare du Nord, May, 1918.* (3) *One of the Warehouses at the Goods Station*
(4) *One of the buildings at the Saint-Frères Works.* (5) *The Rue de la Hotoie.*
(6) *The Rue des Jacobins and the Passage du Commerce connecting it with
the Rue des Trois Cailloux.*

To visit AMIENS,
centre of the itineraries for BAPAUME and PÉRONNE (" THE
FIRST BATTLE OF THE SOMME ") and MONTDIDIER and COMPIÈGNE
THE SECOND BATTLE OF THE SOMME "), see the MICHELIN
Illustrated Guide :

"AMIENS, before and during the War."

# FROM AMIENS TO COMPIÈGNE
## Lunch at Montdidier.

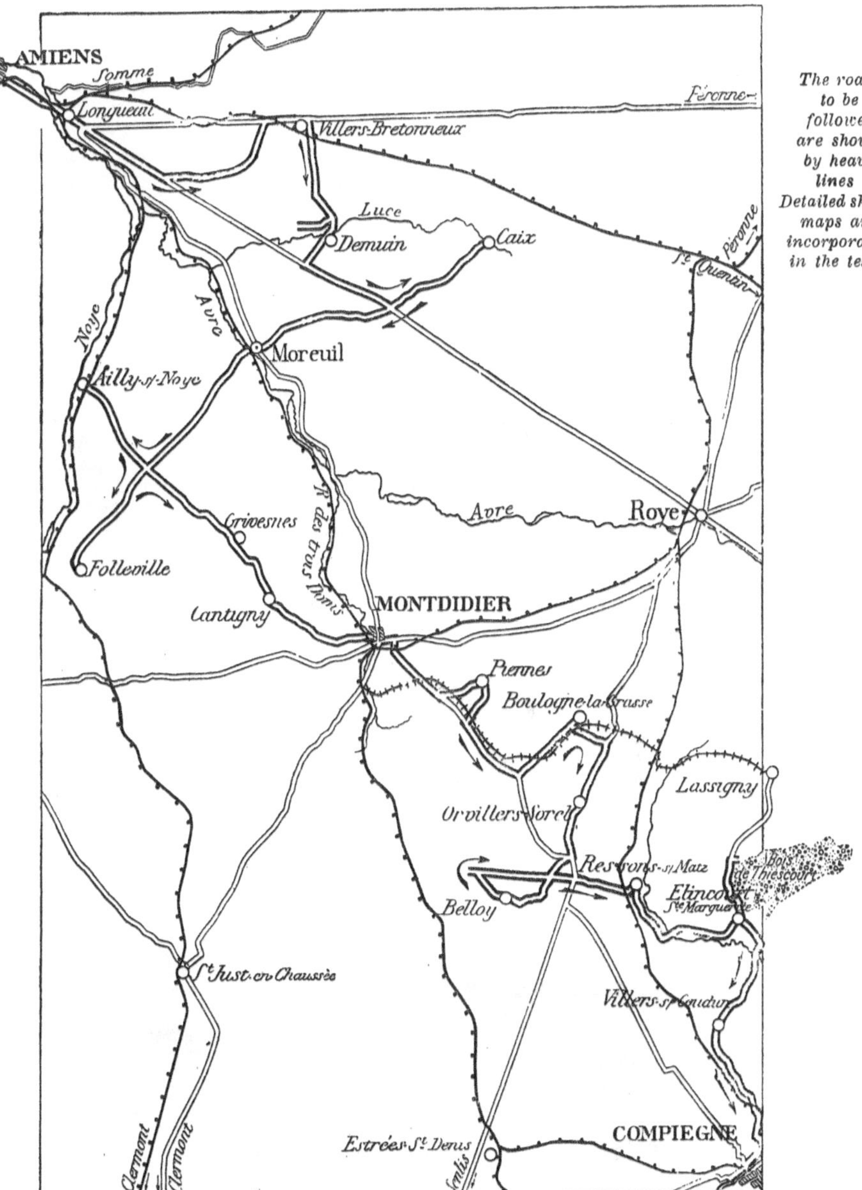

# AMIENS TO COMPIÈGNE

*See route-map, p. 57.*

## From Amiens to Villers-Bretonneux
### via Longueau, Gentelles and Cachy.

*Leave Amiens by Exit V (Michelin Tourist Guide) (Rue Jules-Barni, Chaussée Périgord and N. 35). Cross the railway twice (l.c.) or if preferred, take the road on the right under the railway. Longueau is soon reached.*

The road from Amiens to the crossing over the river Avre, before reaching Longueau, follows the left bank of the Somme. Market-gardens famous for their fertility and known locally as " *hortillonnages* "

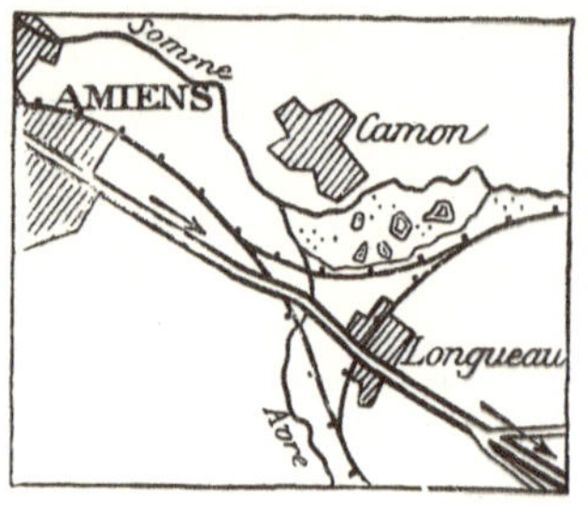

lie in the valley, especially around Camon. Formerly, the river-side *seigneurs* above Amiens, met once a year for wild swan-shooting in the valley of the Somme. The custom died out in the 18th century, poaching having by then exterminated the swans.

It was at Longueau that the Roman roads from Amiens to Rheims and to St. Quentin crossed the river Avre. Gallo-Roman tombstones were discovered in 1848, while excavating near the first bridge at Longueau. In 1590, the Leaguers held the village to ransom, and the Spaniards burnt it in 1636.

*Beyond Longueau, leave the Montdidier road on the right, and keep straight along the road to Roye for 4 1/2 kms. Take the second road on the left, to Gentelles. Gun emplacements, shelters and trenches are met with on both sides of the road. Gentelles Wood is on the right. (See sketch-map, p. 59).*

*Pass through Gentelles village, entirely destroyed. 1 1/2 kms. beyond Gentelles stands* a partly destroyed monument to the memory of the French who fell in the Franco-German War of 1870 *(photo below).*

MONUMENT TO THE FRENCH DEAD OF 1870, AT ENTRANCE TO CACHY.

*Leave the monument on the right, and enter* **Cachy** (completely ruined).

*At the fork beyond Cachy, take the middle road, between the Woods of Aquenne and Abbé, in which are trenches, wire entanglements and shelters. Coming out into the main road from Amiens to Villers-Bretonneux (G. C. 201), take same on the right. (See sketch-map, p. 62).*

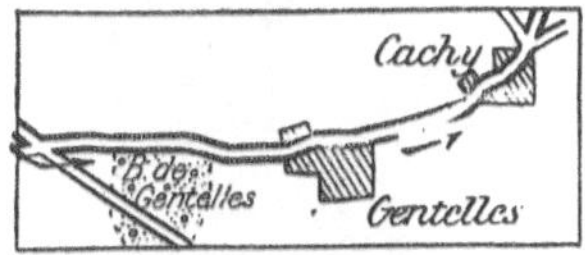



*After passing over the railway,* **Villers-Bretonneux** *is reached.*

VILLERS-BRETONNEUX. — RUINS OF THE VILLAGE AND CHURCH.

VILLERS-BRETONNEUX. THE CHURCH, IN MAY 1918.

Formerly a country village, the cotton-spinning industry later transformed it into a small town. The war has left it in ruins. (*See p. 61.*)

## From Villers-Bretonneux to Moreuil,
### via Demuin, Hill 104, Mézières and Villers-aux-Érables.

*Leave Villers-Bretonneux by the road to Demuin, on the right (G. C. 23).*
*See route-map, p. 62.*

*From Hill 98, 1 km. beyond the railway, near the junction with the road leading to Cachy, and close to a Franco-British cemetery, there is an extensive view of the battlefield around Villers-Bretonneux.*

VILLERS-
BRETONNEUX.
CHURCH
IN NOV. 1918.

STREET
IN
VILLERS-
BRETONNEUX
AFTER
RECAPTURE
OF THE VILLAGE.

FRANCO-
BRITISH
CEMETERY
NEAR
HILL 98.
*In the
background:*
VILLERS-
BRETONNEUX.

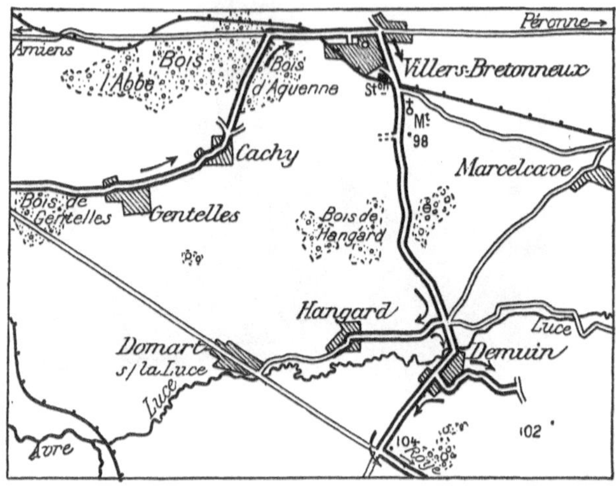



**The Battle of 1870.**

It was around Villers-Bretonneux that on November 27, 1870, part of the battle known as the " Battle of Amiens ", was fought between the Prussians and the French Army of the North.

The French troops, about 10,000 in number, under the command of General Farre, were deployed from the railway (between Villers-Bretonneux and Marcelcave) to Cachy and Gentelles (on the Boves road), and on the high ground dominating the valleys of the Somme, Luce and Avre. The Prussians, under General Manteuffel, far more numerous and better equipped with artillery than the French, debouched from the valley of the Luce and the roads from Péronne and Roye to Amiens, the battle opening on the two wings.

The enemy partly took Cachy and approached Gentelles, but were driven back towards the river Luce, after the brilliant capture of Domart Wood by the French. Cachy, partly abandoned by the French after desperate resistance and heavy losses, was afterwards cleared of the enemy with great dash.

Unfortunately the French line from Cachy to Villers-Bretonneux was too weakly held to stay the Prussians, who got the upper hand in the afternoon and forced the French back. To the enemy's forty guns the French could only oppose sixteen (four batteries), and they were, moreover, short of ammunition.

A Prussian battery, which had succeeded in taking up a position near Cachy, enfiladed the French line. In Villers-Bretonneux, detachments of French Marines fought a violent engagement in the streets, giving ground only step-by-step. The enemy sustained heavy losses and were unable seriously to hamper the French withdrawal towards Corbie and Amiens.

A monument was erected at Villers-Bretonneux, south of the railway, to the memory of the French soldiers who fell in this battle.

Fierce fighting took place in 1918 around the monument, which was completely destroyed.

GERMAN PRISONERS ENTERING VILLERS-BRETONNEUX. (*August* 1918.)

## The Battles of 1918.

Prolonged and violent engagements were fought from March to August, 1918, in the vicinity of Villers-Bretonneux, for the possession of Amiens. The battlefield consisted of a plateau occupied, from northeast to south-west, by Villers-Bretonneux, Abbé Wood, Cachy and Gentelles. This plateau was the last dominating position in front of Amiens. From Villers-Bretonneux, situated on the main road from St. Quentin to Amiens, and ten miles from the latter, the ground slopes gradually down towards the great Picardian City and the confluence of the rivers Avre and Somme.

From March 28 onwards, this plateau was held by Australian divisions, the famous Anzacs, who covered themselves with glory there by staying the Germans. At the beginning of April, the latter attempted to outflank Villers from the north and south, with but little suc-

FRANCO-BRITISH CEMETERY AT " CRUCIFIX CORNER "
ON THE VILLERS-BRETONNEUX-DEMUIN ROAD.

HANGARD VILLAGE, IN RUINS. THE CHURCH IS ON THE RIGHT.

cess. On the 24th, after a bombardment with high explosive and gas shells, lasting the whole of the previous night, they threw four divisions (50,000 men), supported by five tanks each fitted with three guns and a central turret, against the Fouilloy-Cachy front, barely three miles wide. From 7 to 10 a. m., the attacking waves went forward unceasingly in the morning mists. At about 11 a. m., the British had to give way, under an intensely fierce onslaught, and the Germans entered Villers from the north and south.

Clinging to the western approaches of the village, the British, throughout the afternoon and night of the 24th, prevented the enemy from debouching, while their artillery fire made the position practically untenable. Two German battalions only were able to maintain themselves in the cellars and ruins of the houses. In the evening of the

ENTRANCE TO DEMUIN VILLAGE.

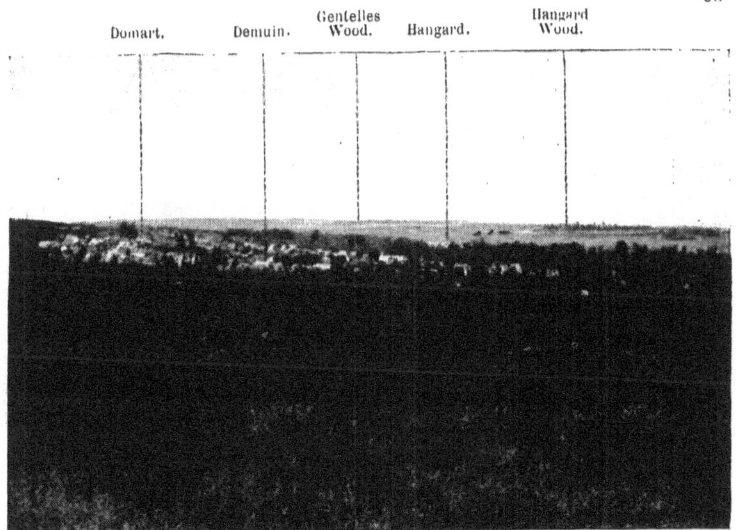


PANORAMA SEEN FROM HILL 102.

25th, while troops of the Moroccan Division recaptured the monument south of the Villers railway, British units debouched from Abbé Wood, and advancing via the ravine north of Villers, Aquenne Wood and the station to the south, surrounded and recaptured the village after a hand-to-hand fight lasting all night. A 3-gun tank and over 700 prisoners were taken. To the south-west, in the vicinity of Cachy and Gentelles, the enemy check was equally severe. On the 24th, a regular battle of tanks took place near Cachy, in which the Germans were routed and Cachy reoccupied. The four German divisions lost the battle, and left the ground covered with their dead.

On May 2, there was again sharp fighting near the Monument, but during the following weeks, the enemy ceased their attacks. The Australians, by local operations, enlarged their positions north-east of Villers-Bretonneux and between Villers and the Somme. On the night of May 23, the enemy violently bombarded Villers, and on the 25th made another powerful effort south of the village, but without success.

*Follow G. C. 23, which runs close to* Hangard *Wood, the trees of which were devasted by the shells.* (*See map, p. 62.*)

*Descend from the plateau to* **Demuin,** *visible at the bottom of the valley of the Luce. There is a large British cemetery on the right. Tourists may here turn to the right as far as* **Hangard.** (*See p. 66.*)

*After visiting the village* (completely devastated), *return to Demuin. Take the main street, then the last street of the village and the uphill road indicated in the sketch-map opposite, to* **Hill 102,** *from which there is a fine view of Demuin, the valley of the Luce, Hangard, Domart and Gentelles Wood* (*photo above*).

*Return to Demuin, and take G. C. 23 to* **Hill 104** (*See map, p. 62*).

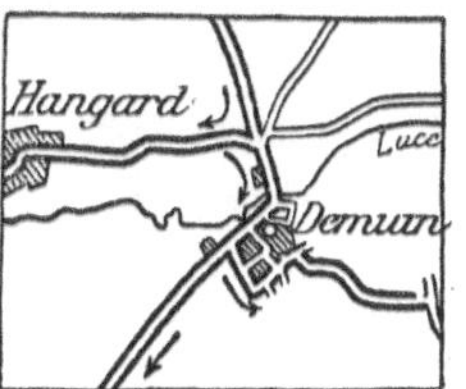

PANORAMA OF THE LUCE VALLEY

### HIll 104.

Hill 104, at the crossing of the Demuin-Moreuil road with the Roye-Amiens road, commands the valleys of the Luce and the Avre.

Hangard and Hangard Wood, seen to the north, were the scene of furious fighting in 1918. This vital position enabled the Germans to hold the river Luce, which they needed to consolidate the Montdidier-Moreuil salient, and for their advance south-east of Amiens.

As early as March 27, units of Debeney's Army, under the command of General Mesple, were pushed south of the Luce in support of the British who were holding the line: Le Quesnel, Beaucourt, Cayeux, Guillaucourt and Proyart. However, on the 28th, the Germans carried Guillaucourt, north of Cayeux, descended to the woods in the Luce Valley, and drove back the British in the neighbourhood of Cayeux. Meanwhile, General Mesple's detachment, in accordance with instructions, stubbornly held their positions on the Caix-Le Quesnel plateau, although unprotected on their left. The first battalions of the French 22nd Division were despatched immediately on arrival to Hangard and Domart, in support of the British. On the 29th, the Germans attacked Demuin on the Luce and forced the Allies to abandon Mézières and to fall back on Moreuil and the Avre.

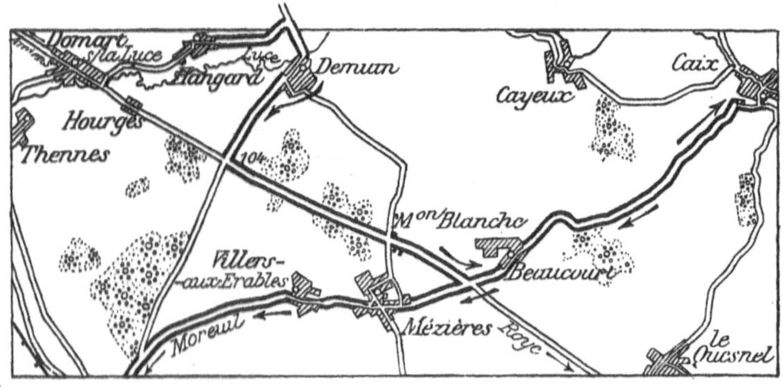

SEEN FROM HILL 104.

On the 31st, they gained a footing in Hangard after prolonged efforts. In the evening and throughout the night they vainly attempted to enlarge their gains to the west. The Franco-British troops repulsed all assaults and prevented the enemy debouching from the village, which the French soon afterwards recaptured in a dashing counter-attack. On April 4, the Germans attempted to turn Hangard from the south and attacked Hill 104. After getting to within 50 yards of it, they were checked at the foot of the hill, and fell back in disorder. They then attempted to slip in along the ravines, but the Allied artillery drove them back with very heavy losses.

On the 6th and 8th, fighting was resumed in the vicinity of Hangard, where the French 29th Division held their ground. On the 9th, Hangard was lost and retaken, together with the cemetery situated about 200 yards east of the village. On the 11th, a fresh German attack was made against the Hangard-Hourges front. The enemy, held before Hourges, gained a footing in Hangard, where the fighting was desperate. On the morning of the 12th, the Germans surrounded the château and occupied the whole of the wood on Hill 104. A single French battalion in the village held out against four German battalions. In the direction of Hourges the enemy was held.

In Hangard Château, the French battalion, although surrounded since 10 a. m., was still holding out at 6.30 p. m., in spite of repeated attacks. At night-fall, a counter-attack by one French and one British battalions recaptured the village and castle, and drove back the enemy to the cemetery. 127 men, 3 officers and 15 machine-guns were captured, and 35 Allied prisoners released. On April 15, before it was relieved, the 29th Division, which had performed prodigies of valour in its efforts to save Hangard, made it a point of honour to clear the village entirely before leaving. One company carried the cemetery in brilliant style. On the 19th, a German effort against the village and wood failed. On the 24th, the fighting was again fiercest around Hangard, which was defended by only one battalion. A whole German division attacked and after carrying the wood boarded the village from the north. At the same time they attacked Hill 104 from the south, at the foot of which they had been held on the 4th.

MAISON BLANCHE. — BRITISH TANKS GOING INTO ACTION.

Enfiladed by machine-guns posted in front of Thennes, the Germans failed to reach that village, but persisted in their efforts against Hangard. After seven furious onslaughts, from 6.30 a. m. to 4.30 p. m., they occupied the cemetery, in which a single company, entirely cut off from all support, held out all that day. Units of the battalion, hard pressed from the north, east and south, shut themselves up with their Commandant in the Château, and made a vigorous defence. Between 3 and 5 p. m., the following message was signalled three times : " *Surrounded in Hangard but still holding out* ". At 6 p. m. the Château was stormed, and the commandant taken prisoner with the remaining survivors. Taking advantage of the confusion caused by the French bombardment among his captors, he escaped with his men and re-entered the castle, where he continued to hold out until nightfall. He was finally captured in the course of another attack.

In spite of their strenuous efforts, the Germans were unable to debouch from Hangard during the night. On the 25th, the French counter-attacked, and after crossing the Luce at various points, reoccupied Verger hamlet, Hangard village, and part of Hangard Wood, repulsing all German counter-attacks.

On the 26th, the 4th Regiment of the Moroccan Division completed the clearing of the wood. Although the British attack on their right was unsuccessful, a battalion of " Légionnaires " succeeded in outflanking the north-eastern corner of the wood, in which they gained a footing. They were followed soon afterwards by a second battalion supported by British tanks which undertook the destruction of the German machine-guns nests. Driven from the wood, the Germans bombarded it heavily with 6in. and 8in. shells, but could not drive out the French. Finally the Germans retreated 2 kms, two of their divisions being thrown into disorder. One of them, which had just relieved the other, suffered such heavy losses that it had to be sent to the rear two days after coming into line. On the 28th, the Germans launched unsuccessful counter-attacks against the wood, which was finally cleared by French Infantry and British tanks. Thereafter, the enemy were unable to make any advance in this region.

*At Hill* 104, *take on the left the road to Roye* (G. C. 203), *and cross*

**Maison Blanche.** *Take the first road on the left (G. C. 28), and skirt the Château of Beaucourt, in the park of which there is a* French cemetery. *Go through* **Beaucourt,** *and keep along the road to* **Caix** (*See map, p. 66*). Saps, battery positions, and a German cemetery are to be seen along the road. Caix is an ancient market-town. Objects dating from the Bronze Age have been discovered there. The 15th-16th century Sainte-Croix Church (*Hist. Mon.*), standing half-way up the hill, is of archæological interest. The famous square belfry on the left is flanked to the top by buttresses surmounted by four low, massive corbel-turrets with bell-shaped roofs. A door in the western front forms a low overhanging arch with accolade-shaped archivolts, ornamented with inset pinnacles.

A large doorway in the façade, comprising two elliptical leaves, is surmounted by high, pointed arcading forming a tympanum. On the first story, a delicate, open-work balustrade recalls that of Tilloloy; above is a fine rose window. The roof was rebuilt on modified lines after the terrible fire of April 1768, which practically destroyed the whole village. The south front doorway dates from 1530. Its arch is ornamented with delicately carved vine-foliage.

The 16th century pillars, without capitals, in the nave, are decorated with finely carved canopies, several of which are mutilated. The present consoles and statues standing against the pillars are unfortunately not the original ones. In the aisles, the brackets on which the springing of the pointed arches rests, are ornamented with figures of persons, lizards and dæmons... The pillars of the choir with their foliate capitals, and the transept and chancel are 14th century. The high altar comprises a reredos. The carved pulpit and confessional are in the Renaissance style. The richly ornamented font has disappeared. A large holy-water basin of unusual shape (truncated cone) is adorned with several black circles.

All the zinc and lead-work was stripped off and taken away by the Germans during the occupation of 1918. The wooden leaves of the entrance door were removed. The building suffered severely from the bombardments. The upper part of the belfry fell down and the stained glass was destroyed. Part of the cornice and the frame-work of the chevet were ruined.

The fortified château of Caix, vestiges of which still remain, was destroyed by fire in 1400.

CAIX CHURCH.

MÉZIÈRES CHURCH.

The village did not suffer greatly from the bombardments.

Caix was captured by the Germans on March 28, 1918, and retaken by the British at the same time as Beaucourt-en-Santerre, on the evening of August 8, i. e., the first day of the British offensive in Picardy.

*Leave the village by the road taken on entering.  Beyond Beaucourt, keep straight on as far as* **Mézières**, *where take the second road on the right to the church (See map, p. 66).*

The village of Mézières was attacked by the Germans, on March 28, 1918, after the withdrawal of the British.  On the 29th, units of the French 133rd Division, which were defending Mézières, were unable to hold the overwhelming numbers of the enemy, who captured the

VILLERS-AUX-ERABLES. — THE RUINED CHATEAU.

village. On August 8, at the beginning of the offensive by Debeney's Army, the village was recaptured by the 42nd Division, while the 37th Division progressed east of Genonville Wood.

*At the church, take the street on the left, then the first on the right* (G. C. 28), *to* **Villers-aux-Erables**. The village was almost entirely destroyed ; its Château is in ruins.

*The road, along which are numerous graves, trenches and shelters, next crosses the plateau,* where the 133rd Infantry and 4th Cavalry Divisions so heroically retarded the German onrush of March 26-28, 1918.

### Moreuil.

Moreuil, *next reached,* was fortified in the Middle-Ages, but to-day nothing remains of the former ramparts. The Château alone is still existent, and is reached by taking *the third turning on the left (See sketch-map opposite).*

· The Château, comprising the ruins of four bastions with very thick walls, was rebuilt in the 14th or 15th century on the site of a previous castle which probably stood near the church. In 1434, it was besieged and captured by the Anglo-Burgundians. In 1588, it was occupied by the Leaguers. In 1636, during the disastrous "Corbie year", it was taken by the Spaniards, from whom the French wrested it shortly afterwards. In 1791, it was pillaged by the people, like the Château of Mailly-Raineval. Ancient cannon from the Château are now in the Museum of Picardy at Amiens. The modern portion, which served as a living apartment, stood between the two western towers, and was built under

THE AVRE AT MOREUIL.

MOREUIL. — THE CHURCH BEFORE THE WAR.

Louis XVIII. It is now in ruins (*photo p. 28*). A large stone cross, which formerly stood before the doorway of the parish church, was removed and erected near the chapel of the Château. This 14th century monument comprised a pedestal of three superimposed stories, and a columnar shaft and cross, slightly more modern than the pedestal. The cross has disappeared, and only part of the pedestal remains.

*Turn back and follow the street straight to* the church.

Formerly the old abbey church of a Benedictine Monastery which stood within the castle walls, it was rebuilt in modern times in 15th century style — except the façade which dates from the latter part of the 16th century — when the place belonged to the Créqui family. The façade (*Hist. Mon.*) bears a great likeness to that of St. Peter's Church at Montdidier. It comprises two large porches, above which

MOREUIL. — THE CHURCH IN 1919.

rose the square tower of the belfry and the gable of the nave.

The left-hand doorway comprises six pointed arches, the third one from the inside being the most richly ornamented. This arch comprises a series of ten carved subjects, each under a canopy.

The right-hand doorway is a replica on a larger scale of the left-hand one.

A Flamboyant gallery runs above the doors. At the base of the belfry, on the northern front, is a beautiful pointed window with rich 16th century ornamentation.

The church was severely damaged during the battles of 1918. The tower was destroyed and the porches were badly mutilated.

The interior collapsed ; the pillars alone remain standing.

MOREUIL CHURCH.

*Turn left into the road which descends to the Avre.* The bridge was destroyed in 1918, and replaced by two wooden ones.

**Morisel** *is next reached, which pass through.* (*See sketch-map, p. 71.*)

BUILDING A BRIDGE ACROSS THE AVRE, NEAR MOREUIL.

MAILLY-RAINEVAL, SEEN FROM THE ROAD TO HILL 103.

# From Moreuil to Montdidier,

## via Mailly-Raineval, Grivesnes and Cantigny.

### Mailly-Raineval and Hill 103

*On leaving Morisel, there is* a large German cemetery, from which a very fine view of Moreuil and the valley of the Avre may be had. *Take the G. C. 14, on the left, as far as* **Mailly-Raineval**, *entering the village by the road on the left. (See sketch-map, p. 77.)*

This village, first known as Raineval, took the name of Mailly-

MAILLY-RAINEVAL. — RUINS OF THE CHATEAU.

MAILLY-RAINEVAL, SEEN FROM THE WEST SIDE OF HILL 103.
*On the right :* THE CHURCH AND CHATEAU ; *in the background :* ARRIÈRE-COUR WOOD.

Raineval in 1744, when it became the property of the illustrious house of Mailly. The Château, in ruins since 1879, was mostly built in the 16th century, on the site of the former castle, destroyed at the time of the *Jacquerie.* The ruins of the Château include a broken tower dating from the end of the 14th century, and substructures still measuring 250 feet in length. The latter, which were severely damaged by the bombardments, used to support the three stories of the imposing Château (*photo opposite*). The village is now a complete ruin.

*200 yards further on, the road leads to the foot of* **Hill 103** *which can be ascended on foot.*

From this hill, there is a fine view of Moreuil Village and Wood, Sauvillers (*to the south-east*) and Arrière-Cour Wood. (*See map, p.* 77.)

On March 26, 1918, the French 133rd Division, brought up in lorries, and the 4th Cavalry Division, had orders to protect the approaches to Moreuil and the Avre, and to join hands with the British, but were forced to give way under the pressure of the enemy's overwhelming numbers. On the 29th, the French 163rd Division had scarcely detrained when it received orders to defend Moreuil, under the direction of the General commanding the 36th Corps, forming the left of Debeney's Army. The attack, led by two German divisions, began on the night of the 29th. Moreuil, as the nearest point to Amiens, was particularly aimed at by the enemy, but the Canadians and French repulsed all assaults. Finally, after changing hands several times, the village was occupied by the Germans who were, however, unable to debouch, although they lost half of their effective strength in their attempts to do so. On April 1st the British, supported by the French, counter-attacked in the woods north of Moreuil.

On April 4th, a violent German effort on the left bank of the Avre, against the 36th Corps, was twice checked, but the enemy finally succeeded, at very heavy cost, in capturing Mailly-Raineval, Arrière-Cour Wood, Morisel and Castel. On April 5; under the command of General Robillot, the French counter-attacked : the 127th, 166th and 59th divisions towards Mailly-Raineval, and the 17th division in the direction of Moreuil. After driving the enemy from Arrière-Cour Wood, they returned to the outskirts of Mailly-Raineval. In front of Sauvillers, where the tanks did good work, they advanced along the plateau. To the west of Castel, in Sénecat Wood, a furious engagement took place, in the course of which the enemy were driven back with a loss of 100 prisoners. On April 17, the French attacked from Mailly to Castel, captured the greater part of Sénecat Wood, gained a footing in Gros Hêtre Wood, reached the outskirts of Castel — bristling with machine-guns — and on the south attained the heights which dominate the Avre, after taking over 650 prisoners, including 20 officers. The same day, a single French battalion thrown against the village of Castel — held by five companies of infantry and two companies of machine-gunners, of the German 389th regiment of shock troops — advanced 1,400 yards, capturing several redoubts, 254 prisoners (including 10 officers), and 31 machine-guns. On this day also, the tanks played a great part in the capture of Sénecat Wood. The commanding officer of a company of tanks personally took over one of the machines, the crew of which had been put out of action. Making straight for Castel, he swept the streets of the village with his machine-gun, then returned safely to the French lines. Another tank, in hot pursuit of a retreating German battery of 77's, penetrated over 600 yards into the enemy's lines, where it broke down. The gallant crew thereupon got out their machine-guns and held off the enemy until their ammunition ran out. On April 24, an enemy attack on Sénecat Wood failed. On May 11. during a violent attack, the Germans temporarily gained a footing in the woods to the southwest of Mailly, but counter-attacks drove them out. On July 12, the French attacked near Castel and to the south-east of Rouvrel, capturing Castel and 500 prisoners. On the 23rd they took Mailly, Sauvillers,

MAILLY-RAINEVAL IN FLAMES.

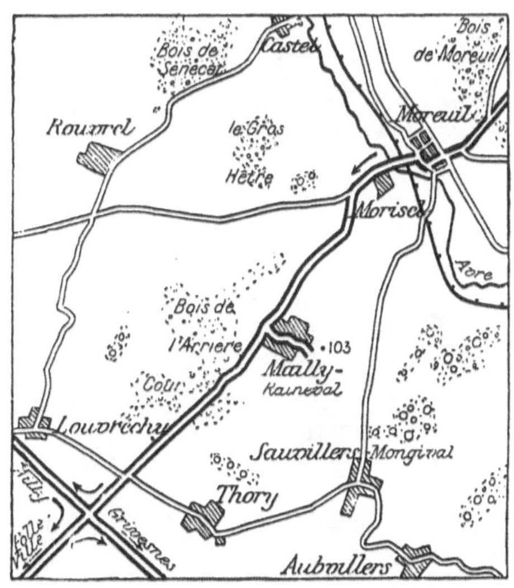


and Aubvillers, capturing 1,800 men, 54 officers, four 77's, 45 minen-werfer, and 300 machine-guns. On August 8, Debeney's offensive cleared Morisel, and the 66th Division captured Moreuil.

*Return to and keep along the road.*

Trenches, saps and battery positions are met with. *After crossing the Louvrechy-Thory road, the Ailly-sur-Noye-Montdidier road is reached. At the crossing, and before taking G. C. 26, on the left, to Grivesnes, tourists interested in archæology should take it on the right to visit the church of* **Ailly-sur-Noye** (5 ½ kms.) *Otherwise, keep straight on to* **Folleville** (4 ½ kms.) (*See sketch-map, p. 79.*)

AILLY-SUR-NOYE. — THE PRÉVOTÉ.

**Ailly-sur-Noye.**

The village of Ailly-sur-Noye used to possess a 13th century church, replaced a few years ago by a new edifice, in which the following portions of the ancient building were retained (under the first window of the right-hand aisle) :

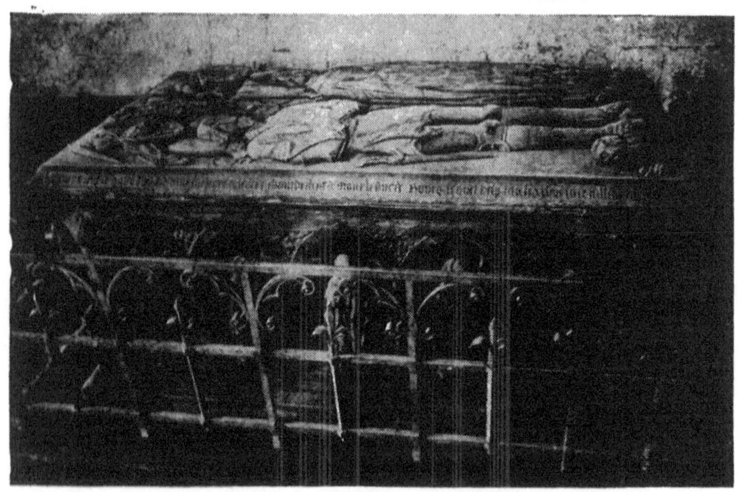

AILLY-SUR-NOYE. — THE TOMB OF THE " BASTARD OF ST. POL ".

1) A bas-relief crowned with pointed trefoil arcading, divided into three compartments, depicting from right to left: *St. Martin cutting his mantle*, *The Crucifixion*, and *The presentation of the donor to Christ, by John-the-Baptist.*

2) The tomb of Jean de Luxembourg, known as the *Bastard of St. Pol*. This tomb (*Hist. Mon.*), comprises a blue-stone sarcophagus, the front of which is ornamented with five mourners, and each end with three other mourners sheltered under arcades. The covering stone is carved with the statues of Jean de Luxembourg and his wife, Catherine de la Tremouille, in demi-relief. Unfortunately, the upper part of these statues is damaged.

### Folleville.

Folleville, with the ruins of its Château and its church, is one of the most interesting places in Picardy, for archæologists. The ruins of the Château (late 14th and early 15th century), situated

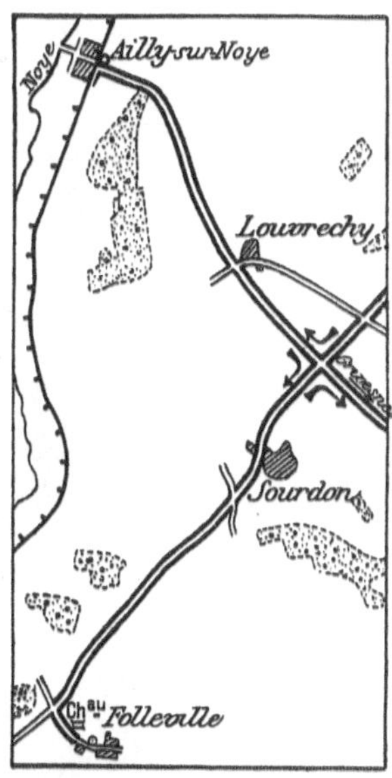


on a hill, from which there is a very extensive view, are most imposing. The corner towers are round; that in the middle of the northern curtain is over 80 feet high, and is first round, then hexagonal, and finally twelve-sided. In proportion as it rises, it overhangs by means of moulded corbels, which bold design gives it a larger diameter at the top than at the base.

The castle, which began to fall into ruins in the 17th century, was further damaged at the time of the Revolution. It is rich in historical

FOLLEVILLE CHATEAU

TOMB
OF
RAOUL
DE
LANNOY
AND
HIS
WIFE.

TOMB
OF
FRANÇOIS
DE
LANNOY
AND
HIS
WIFE.

memories. In 1440, it was taken by the English, under Counts Somerset and Talbot, and served for a long time as their head-quarters. Under Charles IX, the castle served as a meeting-place for the Protestants. Later, the Leaguers had a garrison there. In February 1592, Henri IV fought a battle in the neighbourhood, against the troops of the Duke of Parma. St. Vincent-de-Paul lived there as tutor to M. de Bondi's children, and it was at Folleville that he inaugurated the missions which were the chief aim of the Congregation founded by him.

The church (*Hist. Mon.*) standing near the ruined Château, comprises a late 14th century nave and an early 16th century choir. The latter, intended as a burial chapel for the owners of the castle, is the more richly

FOLLEVILLE CHURCH.

decorated. Its buttresses are surmounted with pinnacles, on one of which is a niche containing a statue of the Virgin. The pointed timber-work vaulting of the nave is among the finest in the *Département* of the Somme, and is decorated with satirical and chimerical carvings. The pulpit is the one from which, on January 25, 1671, St.-Vincent-de-Paul preached the sermon which was the starting-point of his Missions. The wooden seats in the nave' are ancient. The white marble font is girt with the historical chain of the de Lannoy family, connected by four shields bearing the arms of Folleville, Lannoy, Broix and Hangest. It stands on a small pedestal of grey stone, ornamented at the corners with four carved acanthus leaves. The arches of the stone vaulting of the choir rest on small brackets carved with various *motifs*.

Of the two chapels on either side of the choir, that on the left, known as the Virgin Chapel, was used by the owners of the castle. The right-hand one (St. Vincent-de-Paul), is modern in its fittings and decoration (1868).

The choir contains several very famous monuments, the finest being the mausoleum of Raoul de Lannoy and Jeanne de Broix ; the white marble sarcophagus is the work of Italian artists (the *de Portas*) ; the stone niche which shelters the sarcophagus contains delicate French carvings. The whole forms one of the most remarkable works of the Renaissance period. The neighbouring tomb is that of François de Lannoy and Marie de Hangest ; some of the carvings greatly resemble those of Cardinal Hémard de Denonville's tomb in the Cathedral of Amiens.

An ancient stained-glass window near the tomb of Raoul de Lannoy is dedicated to St. Anthony and St. John-the-Evangelist. Above the door of the sacristy are carved marble medallions. The church used to possess a very ancient pall, now in the Museum at Amiens.

FRENCH LINES IN THE QUARRIES AT GRIVESNES.

## Grivesnes.

*Return to the crossing of the Grivesnes, Folleville and Ailly-sur-Noye roads, and take the road leading to* GRIVESNES. (*See sketch-map* p. 84.)

*Before reaching the latter, note the* cemetery of the French 114th Infantry Regiment, *on the right, and a little further on, on the other side*, a quarry containing shelters.

*On entering* Grivesnes, *take the first road on the left to* the CHATEAU — a 17th century pile, comprising a central main building and two wings — in the yard of which are a large shelter and several graves.

GRIVESNES CHATEAU.

The church *is a little farther on.*   Both buildings were severely damaged.
*Return to the road, and proceed towards* CANTIGNY, past the ruins
of a mill which was blown up by the Germans, and the CHAPELLE DE
ST. AIGNAN, near which is a large Franco-German cemetery. (*See map p.*84.)

The chapel is now a heap of ruins.

The village, château and park of Grivesnes now come into view.
The latter lies to the north-east of the village.

On March 28, 1918, the first units of the French 166th Division, on
detraining, took up positions along the Coullemelle-Thory line, while
their artillery was posted on the Grivesnes-Coullemelle line.   On the
29th, the 4th and 5th battalions of the 350th Regiment, which
had already being fighting the two previous days, occupied Grivesnes,
one of them having lost two-thirds of its effective strength.   Reinforced by a few units of Chasseurs and a company of Engineers, this

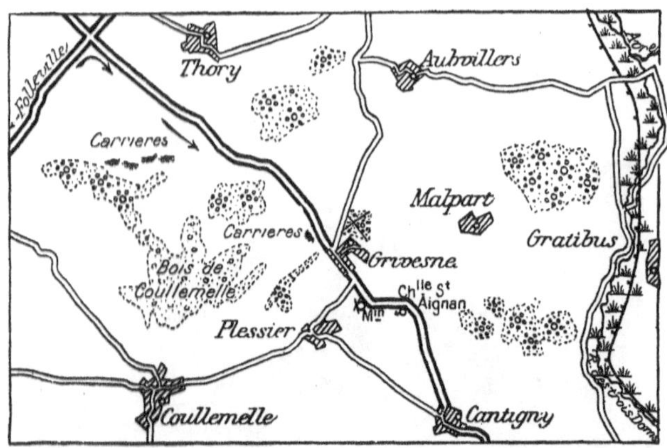



handful of men repulsed five successive assaults next day (March 30), after the fall of Malpart.

On the 31st (Easter Sunday), the enemy attacked with the 1st Division of the famous Prussian Guards. At 7 a. m., French observers saw the storm-waves assembling in the shell-holes to the east and north-east of the park. From 10.30 to 11.30 a. m., the German artillery pounded the French lines with *rafale* fire from 6 in. guns. The German foot-grenadiers advanced by companies, in aligned platoon columns. The first French line was decimated, and broke under the repeated onslaughts. The Germans turned the park from the north and east, and contenting themselves for the time being with surrounding the castle — from which a murderous fire was poured on them — entered the village.

The commanding officer, who had shut himself up in the castle, was using a rifle with his men. At noon, he despatched a cyclist with a report on the situation, to the officer in command of the Divisional Infantry at Plessier. The report ended with the words : *I am in the castle, and shall hold on till death.* The cyclist managed to get through the German lines, crossed Grivesnes — already occupied by the Germans — and delivered the report. All available units were immediately got together and despatched to Grivesnes.

Meanwhile, a reserve battalion at the crossing of the Montdidier and Plessier roads counter-attacked the German Grenadiers who were entering the Rue de Montdidier. While the men were clearing the houses one by one and freeing a number of prisoners, the battalion commander and his cyclist went forward, with two armoured cars, the machine-guns of which scattered the German columns. The Rue de Montdidier was quickly cleared of the enemy and the French entered the Château. At 2.30 p. m., the detachment from Plessier arrived, and the German Grenadiers were quickly driven out of the park. In spite of counter-attacks, the French, with the help of a battalion from a neighbouring regiment, debouched from Coullemelle Wood and fully maintained their positions. The Prussian Guard was thus not only soundly beaten, but also suffered very heavy losses.

The enemy attacked again on April 1 and 3, but without success. On the 4th, the French 67th Infantry Regiment captured St. Aignan

A FEW OF THE HEROES OF THE 350th LINE REGIMENT AND
THEIR COMMANDANT, LIEUT.-COL. LAGARDE.

in the course of a dashing counter-attack, and, in spite of repeated
enemy attempts to reconquer the village, maintained themselves
there. On the 5th the Germans made another powerful but futile
effort against Grivesnes. The 67th Regiment of the line stubbornly
held its own at St. Aignan, while to the east of Grivesnes, the 25th
battalion of Chasseurs repulsed four attacks by two regiments of the
Guard, who were decimated by barrage and machine-gun fire. Later,
the same battalion succeeded in clearing the eastern approaches to
the village. On May 9 the French captured the park, taking 258
prisoners and a large quantity of stores, and beating off all enemy
counter-attacks.

GRIVESNES. — BATTERY OF 8½ IN. MORTARS TAKING UP POSITION.

THE WEATHER-COCK OF THE CHURCH STEEPLE AT GRIVESNES.

*Continue along* G. C. 26 *to* **Cantigny.**

The village and its surroundings were attacked by the Germans at the end of March 1918. Sharp fighting occurred there on the night of the 29th and the whole of the following day. Cantigny fell in the evening of the 30th. On April 4 and 5, a counter-attack in this region by the French 45th Division, drove back the enemy and gave the French the northern and western outskirts of the village, which they were, however, unable to hold. On May 28, the American 1st Division, supported by a regiment of the French 60th Division and a group of tanks, brilliantly carried the village and salient of Cantigny along a 2 km. front, capturing 170 prisoners and a large quantity of stores.

WAYSIDE CROSS AT GRIVESNES.

THE AMERICAN ATTACK ON CANTIGNY, *May 28*, 1918. (*See p.* 39.)

The village was razed to the ground. The ruins of the church and Château may be reached by taking *the street on the left, in the middle of the village.*

FONTAINE-SOUS-MONTDIDIER, in ruins, *is next reached. 3 kms. further on, take the left-hand road to* **Montdidier.** *Skirt the foot of the hill, as far as the Montdidier-Amiens road (N. 35), which take on the right. On entering Montdidier, turn into Rue du Collège which leads to the Esplanade du Prieuré (See p. 98).*

CANTIGNY
ENTRANCE
TO THE
CHATEAU
PARK.

MONTDIDIER. — THE ST. MÉDARD QUARTER.

# MONTDIDIER

*Valiant City, martyrised by the War. After sustaining the fire of the enemy's guns for more than two years, experienced in turn the joys of deliverance and the horrors of a brutal occupation. An important position, bitterly disputed, it suffered total destruction, paying with its ruins the Victory of the Mother-land.*
(Croix de Guerre.)

The town stands at the extremity of the Plateau of Santerre, half-way between Amiens and Compiègne, in the valleys of the Somme and Oise. Rising in tiers, from south to north, on the limestone cliffs, its highest point is occupied by the Palais-de-Justice.

The town probably first grew up around a farm in which, according to tradition, the monks of the Abbey of Corbie kept Didier, King of the Lombards, whose name was given to the town. The first houses sprang up in the fertile valley, whilst a *castrum* was built on the hill. Owing to its situation on an oft-disputed frontier, Montdidier was destined to have a stirring history. Of the fortifications which Philippe-Auguste caused to be erected there, and which were terminated in 1210, nothing remains but a few fragments of walls covered by the gardens. At various periods the town was besieged, pillaged and burnt.

Under Charles VIII and Louis XII the walls were rebuilt and the city's life began anew, only to be disturbed again by war under François I. After repulsing a band of adventurers in 1522, it was besieged in 1523 by 30,000 English and Germans, led by the Duke of Norfolk and Count de Bure. Although a breach was opened in the city's walls, the burghers refused to capitulate. The place had therefore to be carried by storm, and the enemy burnt it on October 29.

MONTDIDIER, SEEN FROM THE MOREUIL ROAD.

After the town had been rebuilt, the Reform quickly gained ground, in spite of persecutions and the burning of Pastor Michel de la Grange.

In 1636, a powerful Spanish army, under the command of Jean de Werth and Piccolomini, captured Roye and summoned Montdidier to surrender. The burghers refused and, almost unsupported, kept the enemy at bay and made a number of successful sorties. A narrow valley on the road to Breteuil has retained the name of " cut-throat ", in remembrance of one of these sorties, during which 200 Spaniards were slain. After a siege lasting 34 days, the approach of the Royal Army compelled the Spaniards to retreat, and Louis XIII thanked the burghers in person for their courage and loyalty .

From that time forward the town lived in peace. Louis XIV often stayed there on his way to Flanders.

On March 19, 1814, the Cossacks, coming from Roye, entered the town.

The next day a large detachment of Cossacks and Prussian Hussars, infantry and artillery, under the Russian Baron de Geismar, took possession and exacted heavy requisitions in kind.

The Cossacks bivouacked in the streets, with their horses in full harness, and cooked their food in the open. An attack by the combined garrisons of Amiens and Beauvais on March 24 drove out the Cossacks, but the latter returned on the 27th, with the intention of plundering and burning the town. In response to a petition from the chief citizens, Baron de Geismar consented not to burn the town, but allowed his soldiers to pillage it for one hour. On the 28th, the

PANORAMIC VIEW TO THE WEST AND SOUTH OF MONTDIDIER

MONTDIDIER, PHOTOGRAPHED FROM AN AEROPLANE.

*On the left: The Three-Doms Stream, crossed by the road followed by the itinerary (see p. 98);*
*In the middle: Place de l'Hôtel-de-Ville; On the right: Place Faidherbe and the Compiègne road.*

SEEN FROM THE ESPLANADE DU PRIEURÉ.

Cossacks withdrew towards Compiègne, to join the Allies in their march on Paris.

After Easter, the Prussians held the garrison at Montdidier and in 1815 a Prussian garrison occupied the town for three months.

On October 15, 1870, the Prussians again appeared before Montdidier, held only by a few regular troops and some National Guards.

After a short bombardment, which caused the death of several citizens, the Prussians entered the town.

CHAPEL BUILT BY THE SOLDIERS IN THE RUINS OF MONTDIDIER.

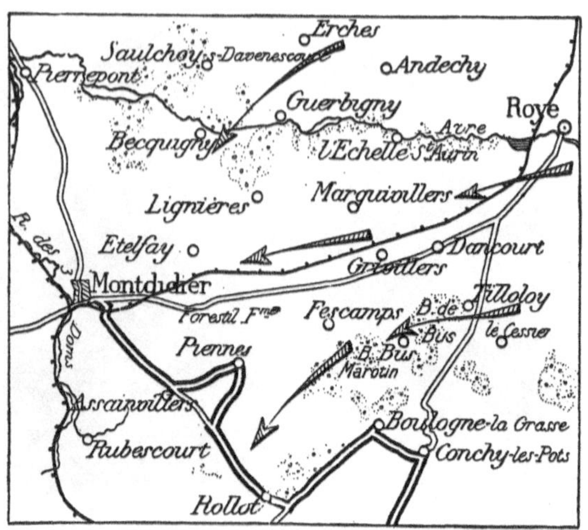

THE ROADS TO BE FOLLOWED ARE SHOWN BY THICK LINES.

## MONTDIDIER IN 1918

Of Montdidier, hardly anything remains but ruins, caused by the terrible battles fought around the town in March-August 1918.

From the end of Rue du Collège, there is a fine view of the whole battlefield : Mesnil-St-Georges and Fontaine-sous-Montdidier *to the west* ; Courtemanche and Framicourt *to the north-west* ; Gratibus, Pierrepont and Contoire *to the north*, and Ayencourt and Monchel *to the south*.

### The German offensive — March 27.

On March 27, the German hordes were held on the French right, but overran the plain on the left, where the lack of natural defences made resistance more difficult. The front-line there was very thin, and the Germans captured Cessier and Tilloloy.

The French 22nd I. D. fell back on Bus, then lost this village and the neighbouring woods. For two hours, the enemy were unable to debouch, being held in check mainly by the fire of batteries in Marotin Wood. Near by, the 22nd Territorials, with a squadron of divisional artillery and two companies of engineers, were thrown into the battle. Fighting stubbornly against odds of ten to one, they retreated only step by step. The Germans advanced only with very heavy loss, and they had scarcely entered Marotin Wood when a concentration of artillery fire scattered them.

Held before the *massif* of Boulogne-la-Grasse, they wedged themselves in between the latter and Montdidier. There was a gap here between the left of Humbert's Army and Debeney's right, then being brought up, and of which only a part, i. e. the 56th Division (Demetz) had taken up its positions. This division, with the 5th Cavalry Division (De la Tour) and two battalions of the 97th Territorials, had to defend a twelve-mile front, extending from Pierrepont to the outskirts of Roye. Attacks by three German Divisions, supported by a powerful artillery, were repulsed.

Throughout the morning, the 69th Battalion of Chasseurs fought along the Echelle-St. Aurin-Dancourt-Grivillers line. The latter village only fell at 12.45 p. m.

After the capture of Erches and Saulchoy the 65th Battalion of Chasseurs held the enemy in check for some time on the Guerbigny line, but on being attacked on the flank by enemy forces which had crossed the Avre beyond Guerbigny, they were compelled to fall back, but only after inflicting very heavy losses on the enemy. This withdrawal brought about that of the 49th Battalion, above Becquigny.

Before Marquivillers, two battalions of the 105th line Regt. held their ground for a long time, and withdrew only after being overwhelmed. Fighting rearguard actions, they fell back on the crest south of Lignières, then to the plateau east of Etelfay. A battalion of the 132nd line Regt., which had been unable to reach Fescamps, fought with the Territorials of the 97th between Piennes and Forestil Farm. At 3 p. m., a battalion of the 132nd was thrown against Etelfay which had been captured by the Germans, thus enabling two battalions of the 106th and one of the 132nd to reform on the plateau to the west, where they kept the enemy in check until 6.30 p. m.

South of Montdidier, the enemy advanced rapidly towards Rollot and Rubescourt.

The defence of Montdidier was abandoned, and the enemy entered the town at 6.30 p. m. The 56th I. D. and the 5th Cav. Div. reformed to the west of Montdidier and the Avre, without losing a single gun.

### The Enemy's Advance held.

In the evening, the French held the line: Ayencourt, Mesnil-St.-Georges, Gratibus, Pierrepont and Contoire. General de Mitry (6th Corps) gave orders to hold at all costs the line of hills which dominate the Three-Doms stream on the west, between Pierrepont and Domfront. The 56th Div. defended the line Framicourt, north of Courtemanche and Domfront.

SAVING THE TOWN RECORDS OF MONTDIDIER.

### March 28.

On the morning of the 28th, the German 9th Div. entered Courtemanche, Framicourt and Fontaine-sous-Montdidier, scattered the units of Engineers who were holding the road to Mesnil, then occupied Mesnil, Ayencourt and Monchel.

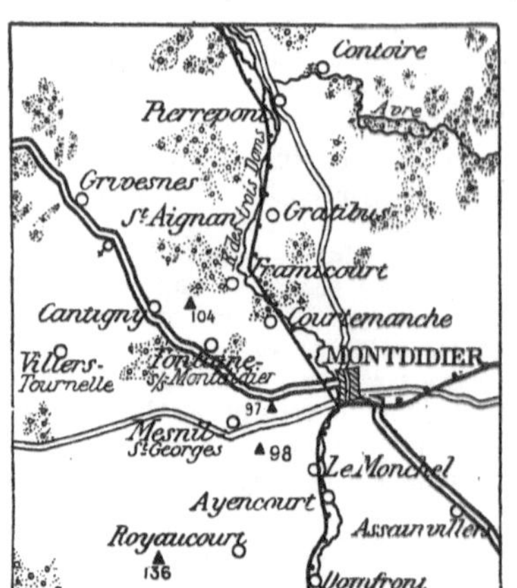


The 56th Div. immediately counter-attacked. While a battalion of the 132nd Regt. recaptured Fontaine-sous-Montdidier, and the 65th Battn. of Chasseurs advanced in the wood and on the hill near Mesnil, the 3rd Battn. of the 132nd, supported by a Battn. of the 350th, drove back the enemy to Mesnil and Monchel, and carried these villages. On the right, General Humbert's Army recaptured Assainvillers.

### March 29.

On the 29th, the 56th Div. received orders to advance as far as the railway, between Courtemanche and Monchel. The attack was launched at 6 p. m., at the very moment chosen by the enemy for their own attack. The fighting at once became very desperate. On the left, a company of the 69th Battn. of Chasseurs succeeded in entering Framicourt, but was overwhelmed and partly taken prisoners. The 49th Battn. of Chasseurs, after advancing as far as the Chapelle de St. Pierre, west of Courtemanche, was outflanked and forced to withdraw beyond Fontaine-sous-Montdidier. The 65th Battn. of Chasseurs and the 3rd Battn. of the 132nd Regt. progressed to the east of Mesnil, as far as Hill 97, but were decimated by a violent artillery and machine-gun barrage, and had to fall back.

### March 30.

At dawn, on the 30th, after a violent artillery preparation, a fresh German attack was launched. To the north, in front of Fontaine-sous-Montdidier and Hill 104, the 49th Battn. of Chasseurs, supported by units of the 54th Regt., repulsed seven assaults.

Two German air-squadrons having swept the French lines with machine-gun fire, the attack was renewed with fresh troops, but without result. At 3.45 p. m., a new attack by strong enemy columns succeeded in turning the exhausted French forces on both flanks. To avoid being surrounded, the French fell back on the crest east of Villers-Tournelle, and clung desperately to their new positions. On that day, they threw over 1,500 grenades and fired over 50,000 cartridges. From Mesnil to Royaucourt, the battle was equally desperate. The German 9th Division had orders to push forward as far as Hill 136, i. e. 2 1/2 kms. south-west of Royaucourt.

In front of Mesnil, the French 106th Regt. broke four attacks in the morning, but at about 5 p. m., the French left having given way under a terrific bombardment, the Germans reached the northern

MONTDIDIER.
RUE
BECQUEREL.
(See p. 98.)

outskirts of the village. The French only abandoned the village, in flames, at 6.30 p. m., taking up fresh positions 200-300 yards in the rear.

On the right, the Germans took Monchel and Ayencourt, but were unable to debouch, which prevented them from reaching the south-western outskirts of Mesnil and the approaches to Royaucourt.

At 7 p. m., a counter-attack by units of the 153rd Regt., a battn. of cavalry on foot, a section of armoured-cars, and a group of artillery took the enemy by surprise. Ayencourt and Monchel were recaptured, and the French line advanced from Monchel to Hill 98.

Exhausted by their efforts and heavy losses, the enemy now consolidated their slight gains.

The French 56th Div. had fought unceasingly for five days and lost the greater part of its effective strength, but had fixed the enemy.

MONTDIDIER.
RUE
BECQUEREL
IN 1919.

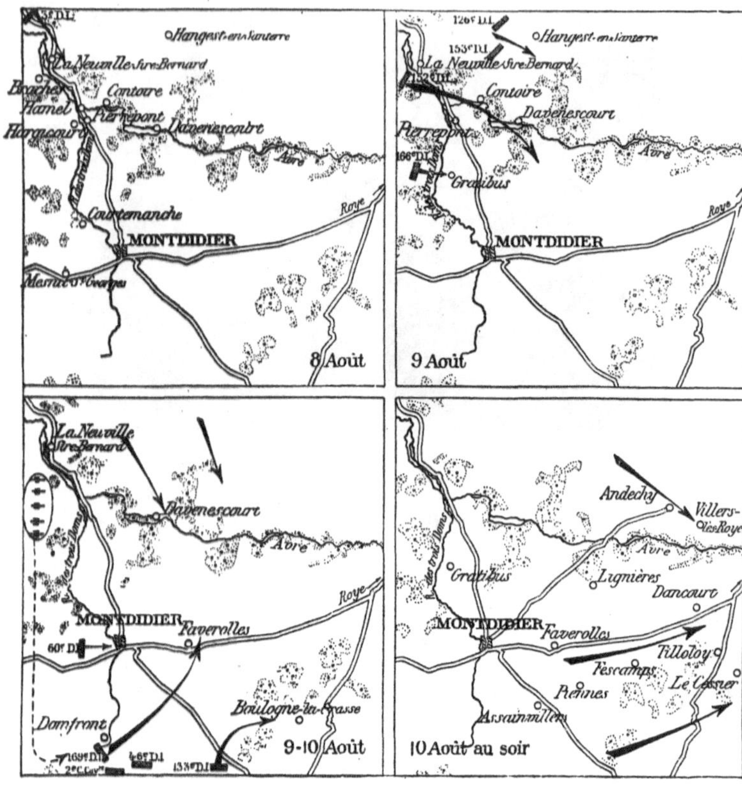



LIBERATING MONTDIDIER.<br>
The front on August 8th. (morning) and 10th (evening).

### The Liberation on Montdidier. (*August* 8-10, 1918.).

During the following months the enemy remained on their positions, the sector being disturbed only by local attacks and raids on either side. In the region of Mesnil-St.-Georges, held mainly by the 60th Div., the extreme German right broke down during the offensive of June 9 against the resistance of the French. In front of a single company of the 248th line Regiment, over 200 German dead were counted.

On August 1, the enemy made many unsuccessful efforts in the neighbourhood of Mesnil. From August 3, the French progressed slowly to the east of the village, and prepared starting positions for Debeney's offensive of August 8. On the 4th the Germans, sensing the coming attack, abandoned part of their positions. The French occupied Braches, gained a footing in Hargicourt, and reached Courtemanche.

On August 8, the 3rd Div. of the 9th Corps crossed the Avre to the north, captured and enlarged the bridgehead of Neuville-Sire-

Bernard and occupied the western outskirts of Contoire and Hamel. The 9th Corps was then replaced by the 10th, the three divisions of which were in the line: the 152nd and 166th behind the Doms stream, and the 60th in front of Montdidier. On the morning of the 9th the 152nd Div., instead of attempting to cross the marshy stream, inclined to the left, crossed at Neuville-Sire-Bernard, and thus enabled the 166th Div. to force the passage by a frontal attack opposite Gratibus. While the 126th and 153rd Div. carried Hangest village and plateau, the 152nd Div. advanced to Contoire and Pierrepont. The 166th Div., which had met with great difficulty in crossing the Doms stream, was unable to gain a footing on the plateau to the east. Montdidier, already outflanked from the north, was now being turned from the south. General Debeney

GERMAN PRISONERS PASSING THROUGH MONTDIDIER (1918).

rapidly transferred his artillery from his left to his right, and began a new attack. The 60th Div. advanced against Montdidier, and the 169th made a north-easterly thrust towards Faverolles, to cut the Montdidier-Roye road, the enemy's main line of retreat. The 133rd Div. attacked eastwards, to mask the *massif* of Boulogne-la-Grasse and cover the flank of the offensive. Behind followed the 46th Div. and 2nd Cavalry Corps, in readiness to exploit any gains.

The attack was a complete success. In the evening, from Faverolles to Piennes, Montdidier was turned from the south. Assainvillers, Piennes and Faverolles were recaptured, and the enemy fell back along the Montdidier-Andechy road, which their desperate resistance before Gratibus had enabled them to keep open. During the night

MONTDIDIER. BUILDING A BRIDGE IN FRONT OF THE STATION.

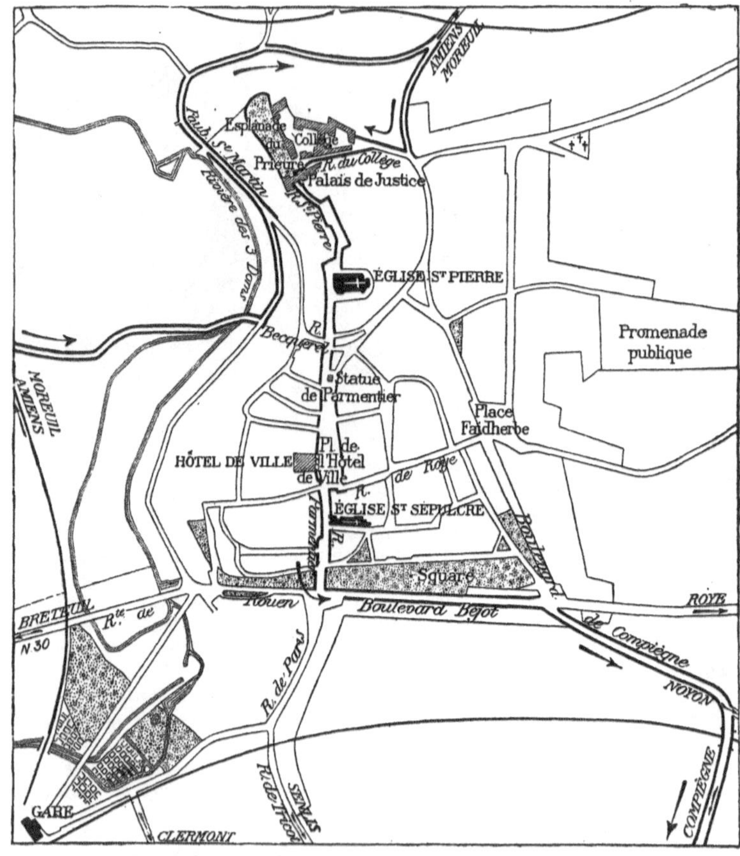


*The roads to be followed are indicated by thick lines and arrows.*

they evacuated Montdidier in the greatest confusion. While the French were entering the town, which was entirely in their possession by noon on the 10th, the whole of Debeney's forces thrust eastwards : the 47th and 56th Div. advanced to the east of Villers-les-Roye, the 166th from Gratibus to Lignières, the 60th to the outskirts of Dancourt, the 46th to the east of Tilloloy, the 133rd to the north-east of Fescamps, and the 169th to before Cessier. Montdidier was now largely cleared.

## A VISIT TO MONTDIDIER.

*Abutting on the Esplanade du Prieuré is* the BENEDICTINES' PRIORY which, before the war, was a college. *Opposite is* the PALAIS-DE-JUSTICE. These two buildings suffered severely from the bombardments.

The **Palais-de-Justice** was built on the site of the old Château of the Counts of Montdidier. The entrance was all that remained of the Château at the beginning of the 14th century. The remains of this door were used in the construction of the building known as the SALLE DU ROY.

MONTDIDIER.
THE PALAIS-
DE-JUSTICE.
(1919.)

The Salle du Roy is built over a vaulted passage, situated opposite the Esplanade du Prieuré.  To the west, an imposing gable rises above the cliffs, its thick walls reinforced in the centre by an enormous buttress, at the northern corner by a smaller buttress, and at the southern corner by an octagonal turret.

The entrance to the Palais-de-Justice is below the vaulted passage.  On the first story, the Entrance Hall and the corridor leading to the Audience Chamber were decorated with six large Brussels tapestries, believed to be work of Henry Reydams (17th century).  Made originally for the town of Douai, they were taken from the Château of Ferrières — pulled down in 1809 — in the Department of Oise. The subjects, taken from the Book of Exodus, depicted : *The Crossing of the Red Sea ; the Hebrews glorifying God ; Gathering Manna; Moses striking the Rock ; Making the Golden Calf ; Worshipping the Golden Calf.*  The 1st, 3rd and 4th were faithful reproductions

THE PALAIS
DE-JUSTICE
IN 1917.

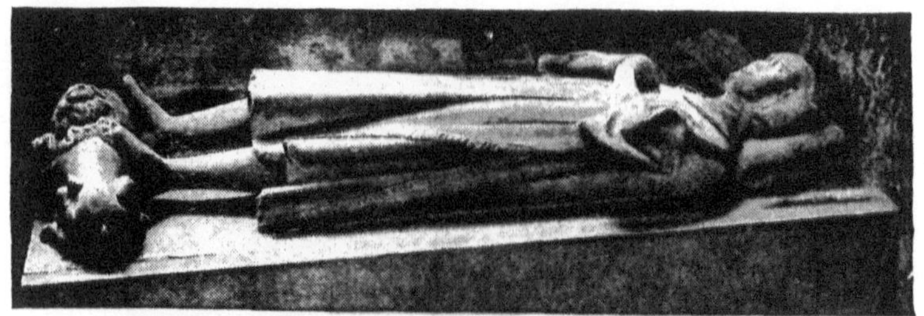

THE TOMB OF RAOUL DE CRÉPY.

of tapestries in the Cathedral of Chartres, said to have been made after drawings by Raphael.

The other public buildings of Montdidier stood in the main road which divides the town from north to south into two unequal parts. The first of these was the **Church of St. Pierre** (*Hist. Mon.*) *reached by passing under the archway of the Palais-de-Justice and following Rue St. Pierre.*

Of this church hardly anything remains except the walls and débris. Portions of the building were 14th century, but most of it dated from the 16th century. The tower, now in ruins, was added in 1742. The doorway was the most remarkable part of the building. The plans were the work of Chaperon (1538), the master-mason of Beauvais Cathedral. The style is a combination of flamboyant Gothic (central dividing pillar, archways, springing of the archways, and niches with socle and canopy at the base of the main pillars), and Renaissance (voluted niches and trefoiled bell-turrets, at the top of the pillars). At the top of the accolade-shaped arch was a shield bearing the arms of France, surrounded by St. Michael's collar, the three crescents

THE INTERIOR OF ST. PETER'S CHURCH.

MONTDIDIER CEMETERY (*north-east of the town*).
*See Itinerary, p. 98.*

of Henri II, and a monogram combining the "H" of Henri II, the double "D" of Diane de Poitiers, and the double "C" of Catherine de Médicis. The side-walls of the church are sustained by buttresses. In accordance with a custom fairly common in Picardy, each bay of the side-aisles had its own separate roof forming a right-angle with that of the great nave. The interior, with its three naves, massive pillars and low 15th century vaulting — lower at the choir end than ne r the doorway — appeared somewhat heavy in style.

At the bottom of the left aisle, a reclining statue was said to depict

PLACE FAIDHERBE.
(*At the end of Rue de Roye, which comes out into Place de l'Hôtel-de-Ville. See p. 98*).

THE STATUE OF PARMENTIER (1914).

Count Raoul de Crépy, and to have formed part of the tomb which the Count had built in the 11th century, while still alive. This statue escaped destruction during the Revolution, and was deposited in the church in 1862. As a matter of fact, it probably dates from the 13th or 14th century, and does not represent Raoul de Crépy.

In the adjoining chapel is a *Burial Scene* comprising seven figures grouped around that of Christ. As in the Tomb of St. Germain-les-Fossés at Amiens, Mary Magdalene occupies the centre of the group, whereas this place is usually reserved for the Virgin.

The font (probably 11th. century) is the oldest known specimen of the type used in Picardy between the 11th and 16th centuries. The

THE STATUE OF PARMENTIER AND A CORNER OF THE TOWN, IN 1919.
*looking towards St. Peter's Church, seen behind. Tourists follow the road on the left.)*

low, square basin rests on five supports, the principal one being in the centre, the other four lesser columns at the corners. The columns, originally in stone, were replaced in the course of time by wooden ones. A belt ornamented with eight heads of rather primitive design runs round the basin. The rest of the decoration, much defaced, includes two entwined heads, grapes, and doves drinking out of a vase.

The tomb, said to be that of Raoul de Crépy, the " Burial Scene " and the font are believed to lie buried under the débris.

The organ loft, composed of the remains of fine Renaissance wood carving of uncertain origin, was destroyed.

*Keep along Rue St. Pierre to Place de la Croix-Bleue, in which stood* the STATUE OF PARMENTIER (by Malknecht), erected in 1848. Only

MONTDIDIER. — THE HOTEL-DE-VILLE.

the pedestal remains. Parmentier, who introduced and popularized potato growing in France, was a native of Montdidier.

*Rue de la Croix-Bleue leads to Place de l'Hôtel-de-Ville. On the right stands* the modern **Hôtel-de-Ville** which replaced the old Louis XIII building and a Renaissance house on its right. The automaton bell-striker of the old tower, known as JEAN DUQUESNE, which used to strike the hours with a hammer, was erected on the top of the new belfry.

*Rue Parmentier is next reached, at the entrance to which is* the 16th century **Church of the Holy Sepulchre.**

Its modern flamboyant Gothic doorway replaced the old portal which, jutting out in front of the church, was ornamented with a hanging garden. On this side, the square tower of the belfry only is ancient. The five-sided chevet overlooks the small court of the presbytery.

The interior comprises a central and two side naves. Only the vaulting of the choir remains.

At the end of the right aisle is an *Entombment* (1549-1582), a gift of the De Baillon family. The Tomb, which was protected during the war, comprises *The Burial Scene* and an *Ecce Homo* at the top of the

MONTDIDIER. — RUE PARMENTIER AND THE CHURCH OF ST. SEPULCHRE (1914).

arch over the former. The latter group was finished long before the other one, and is more natural and of finer finish than that of the Tomb. The figures kneeling at the praying-desks on the front of the Tomb represent Pierre de Baillon and his wife, Marguerite de la Morlière. At the other end of the right aisle stood the baptismal font (1539), mutilated and covered with whitewash in 1870. The church

THE CHURCH OF ST. SEPULCHRE IN 1919.

CHURCH OF ST. SEPULCHRE. THE CHANCEL.

of La Boissière possesses an identical font dating from the same period, but much better preserved. The font probably lies buried under the débris. In the font chapel there is a stone bas-relief (protected

THE INTERIOR OF THE CHURCH OF ST. SEPULCHRE.
(*Seen from the Chancel, near the Porch*).

MONTDIDIER. — THE LOWER TOWN, SEEN THROUGH A SHELL-HOLE
IN THE CHURCH OF ST. SEPULCHRE.

during the war), said to have come from the old church. It was consecrated to the Virgin, who is seen receiving the benediction of the Eternal Father. The carvings and inscriptions around the Virgin, symbolically recalling the principal episodes in her life, are taken from the Song of Solomon. Unfortunately, this bas-relief was daubed over in 1870, and some of the carvings, particularly *Les trois enfants qui pissent*, were mutilated because of their realism.

*Go down Rue Parmentier, then turn left into Boulevard Béjot, in the direction of Compiègne.*

## From Montdidier to Cuvilly,

### via Assainvillers, Piennes, Rollot, Boulogne-la-Grasse, Conchy-les-Pots and Orvillers-Sorel.

*Follow Boulevard Béjot, then take Boulevard de Compiègne, on the right, and a little further on, N. 35, also on the right, to* **Assainvillers,** *entirely razed. Take the second road on the left and cross the light railway, 0 km. 700 beyond which are several lines of trenches. Take the left-hand street, which leads straight to the church and village of* **Piennes.** *(See sketch-map opposite.)*

ASSAINVILLERS IN RUINS.

### Piennes.

The church of Piennes (*Hist. Mon.*) dating from the end of the 15th or beginning of the 16th century, was a remarkable structure.

The tierce-point doorway comprised two round-arched bays, with a blind Flamboyant tympanum. The dividing pillar was surmounted by a statue of the Virgin resting on a crescent.

Between the doorway and the buttresses framing it, an elaborate Gothic canopy sheltered an empty niche on either side. The front of

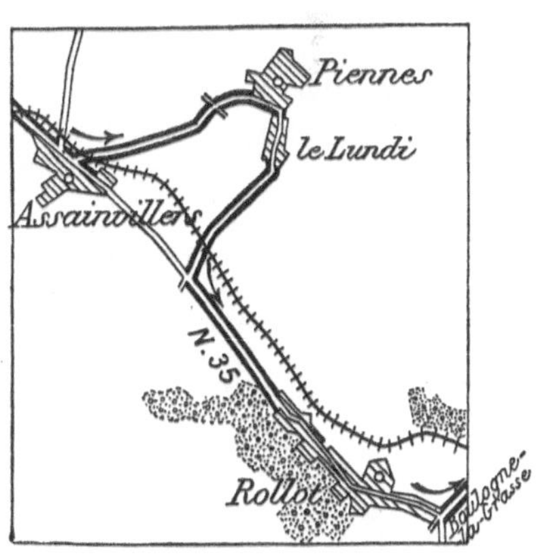

ASSAINVILLERS CHURCH.

PIENNES CHURCH.

each buttress was ornamented with a niche under a Gothic canopy containing mutilated statues of St. Catherine and St. Marguerite.

The side-aisles were very picturesque with their five gables and five separate roofs at right-angles to that of the great nave.

The vaulting is said to have been designed by Jean Vaast, one of the architects of Beauvais Cathedral. The pretty 16th century ·font was ornamented with angels' heads and fantastic figures arranged alternately and linked together by festoons of leaves. The remarkable churchwardens' bench of carved wood in Renaissance style was one of the finest in the *Département* of the Somme. The wood-work of the pulpit dated from the same period and was in the same style.

The church was almost entirely destroyed in 1918, but a portion of the door-way and a buttress with a niche still remain. The gables of the side-aisles, three of which have retained their roofing, are still standing.

ROLLOT. — RUE DE L'ÉGLISE.

THE ROAD FROM ROLLOT TO BOULOGNE-LA-GRASSE.

The font near the entrance, on the left, is partly hidden under the débris. The pulpit was destroyed by the falling tower and vaulting.

*Leave Piennes and pass through the hamlet of* **Le Lundi**. Trenches may be seen alongside the railway. *Take the Montdidier-Compiègne road on the left to* **Rollot**, where Antoine Gallant, the Oriental writer and translator of the French version of " The Arabian Nights ", was born in 1646. Of the monument erected to his memory in the village, only the pedestal remains.

*On leaving Rollot, take* G. C. 27 *on the left;* the CHATEAU OF BAINS, in the woods skirting the road on the left, was greatly damaged during the fighting. *Keep straight on to* the church of **Boulogne-la-Grasse**.

CHATEAU OF BAINS.

BOULOGNE-LA-GRASSE. — THE RUINED CHURCH.

## Boulogne-la-Grasse.

Boulogne-la-Grasse is situated on the top and along the middle slopes of a kind of small broken *massif*. Before the War, the village consisted of a number of independant quarters intersected by picturesque, winding streets, the whole hidden from view by gardens and orchards.

THE CHOIR OF THE ABOVE CHURCH.

BOULOGNE-
LA-GRASSE.
CHATEAU
(1914).

The church, access to which is gained by a flight of 34 steps, over-looks the main street.  The choir alone is ancient.

*Take the street on the left of the church, then the first on the left which leads to the top of the massif overlooking the village.*

The moats surrounding the site of the old fortified Château are still visible.  The latter was replaced by a modern Château, now in ruins.

The telegraph-station, which used to stand on the top of the hill, to the west of the village, was destroyed by the Prussians in 1814.

From here, there is a fine panorama of the battlefield.  On March 27, 1918, the Germans attacked Boulogne and the villages to the east, i. e. Conchy-les-Pots, Roye-sur-Matz, and Canny-sur-Matz, held by part of the French 38th Division which had been brought up to reinforce the 62nd Division, seriously depleted by several days' fighting.  The Germans captured Boulogne and Conchy, but the next

THE
COURTYARD
OF THE
CHATEAU
(1918).

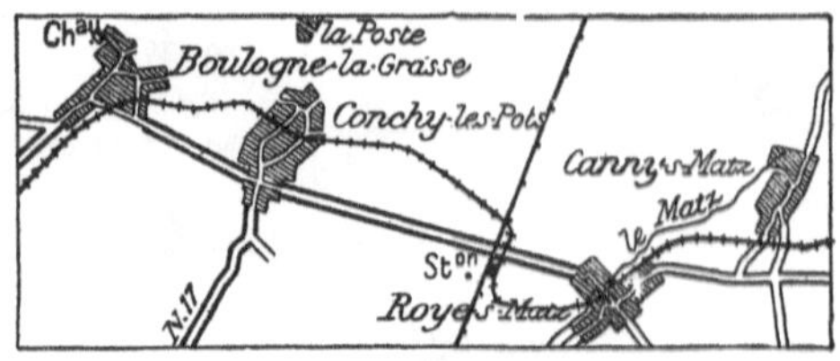


day (28th), the French counter-attacked and retook both villages. Having, after two unsuccessful assaults, gained a footing in Canny - sur - Matz, the enemy launched repeated violent counter-attacks against Conchy and Boulogne, reoccupying the former, but recapturing only part of the latter. On the 29th, the French progressed beyond Boulogne and again reached the outskirts of Conchy without, however, being able to capture Canny or dislodge the Germans from the eastern part of Boulogne. That night, Boulogne was crushed by the French artillery and made practically untenable, but on the 30th, the German offensive, debouching from Conchy, drove back the French who were occupying the *massif*. During the following months, the Germans organized a line of support in this region known as the " Rheinlandstellung ". General Humbert's offensive of August 10, freed the entire *massif*. The same evening the line ran through Orvillers, Boulogne-la-Grasse, La Poste, north of Conchy, through Conchy-les-Pots and the railway-station of Roye-sur-Matz. On the 11th, in spite of fierce counter-attacks, the French reached the wood north of La Poste, Hill 81 to the east of Roye-sur-Matz, and the outskirts of Canny and La Berlière. On the following days, their advance definitely freed the region. Canny was re-occupied on the 17th.

*Return to the church, keeping straight on as far as the first road on the left* (G. C. 27) *which leads to* **Conchy-les-Pots**. *Before reaching this village*, a Franco-German cemetery *will be seen on the right. A little further on, turn left. At the fork, the left-hand road leads to* the ruins of the parish church dating from the 11th (square choir), 12th and 15th centuries. The church was practically razed. *The road on the right leads to the* St. Nicaise Chapel, *situated immediately beyond the light railway.* This chapel contained fine 15th or 16th century

CONCHY-LES-POTS, A CORNER OF THE RUINS.

stained-glass windows, depicting the story of St. Nicaise, which were placed in safety during the War.

*Return to the entrance to the village. By G. C. 27, on the left, tourists may proceed to* **Roye-sur-Matz,** *whose* church (*Hist. Mon.*) was partly 12th century. It was rebuilt in the 16th-17th centuries, except the doorway, nave, northern transept and tower which were in a remarkably good state of preservation. Previous to the offensives of 1918, the church had been for three years in the firing line, and was seriously damaged between 1914 and 1917. Its ruin was completed in 1918. A few fragments of walls belonging to the chevet are all that remain.

*From Roye-sur-Matz return to Conchy-les-Pots, where take the left-hand (paved) N. 17 to* **Orvillers-Sorel.** *On the left, between Conchy-les-Pots and Orvillers-Sorel, is* the village of BIERMONT, which was desperately defended by the French 62nd Division on March 30, 1918.

ROYE-SUR-MATZ. — THE CHURCH.

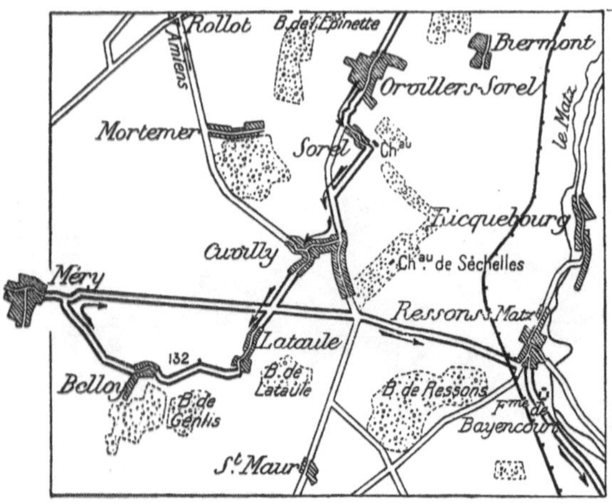


This district suffered severely from the fierce fighting of March-August 1918. On March 30 two German divisions, including one of the Guard, attacked Orvillers-Sorel, defended by a portion of the French 38th Div., the 4th Regt. of Zouaves and the 8th Regt. of Tirailleurs, the heroes of Douaumont, Hurtebise and La Malmaison. These two regiments, overwhelmed by numbers, were forced to fall back, but only after desperate fighting. Units of the 4th Regt. of Zouaves, greatly outnumbered and cut off, fought to the last man. Others managed to cut their way through, falling back only to reform and counter-attack, sometimes without an officer. As far as the northern outskirts of Orvillers, the ground was defended, inch by inch, and the enemy were unable to enter the village. During the night, the 4th Regt. of Zouaves reformed in the ruins, an on the following day (31st) counter-attacked between 1.30 and 2.30 p. m.. reconquering Epinette Wood and taking a number of prisoners. Until May 3, when they were relieved, they maintained their positions. On April 12 and May 11, the French delivered two local attacks and progressed

ORVILLERS-
SOREL
CHURCH
IN RUINS.

to the nortn-west of Orvillers. On May 12 and 14, a German attack against the new positions failed with heavy losses. On August 10, the 34th Corps of Humbert's Army cleared Orvillers-Sorel, and captured the " Gothenstellung ", which formed the third main fighting line of the German defences.

*Beyond the village, a small chapel is passed, on the right, the tourist coming out opposite* **Sorel Château** (late 17th century), *which stands* in a closed park. The Château was seriously damaged during the attacks.

*Take the avenue facing the Château,* which was bordered with trenches, *then N. 17 on the left, to* **Ouvilly.**

This village is situated on the old Flanders road, formerly used by the stage-coaches. The latter used to stop at the Post-House, the old buildings of which were still standing before the War. The church, heavy in style, probably dates in part from the end of the 16th century. Only the walls and tower remain.

*To reach the church take Rue de Matz, on the right, and on reaching the square, bear to the left.*

## Belloy Plateau.

*To reach* Belloy Plateau, on which violent fighting took place in June 1918, *keep straight on the road from Cuvilly to* **Lataule**.

The church of Lataule, although modern, has retained some of the windows of the 15th century edifice. Opposite, stands the Château, built at the end of the 17th century, after the Spanish wars. Of the old Château, destroyed in the 17th century, traces still remain near to the road.

*Turn to the right, skirting the park of the Château, to reach* **Hill 132**, on which are a cemetery, an observation-post, and some trenches.

From there, the view extends over Belloy and Méry to the west, Cuvilly to the north, Lataule and Lataule Wood to the east, Genlis Wood to the south, and St. Maur to the south-east. The Germans gained a footing on this bare plateau on June 10, 1918, capturing the villages of Lataule, Méry, Belloy, St. Maur and Cuvilly, after a fierce

LATAULE.
THE
CHATEAU
IN RUINS.

battle lasting two  days, in which they engaged large forces.  Méry especially, was fiercely disputed and changed hands twice that day. On the following day (11th), the Germans had scarcely installed themselves on the newly conquered ground, when they were thrown into confusion and defeated by the sudden counter-attack of a group of divisions under General Mangin.  All available tanks had been assembled within twelve hours, in support of this counter-attack, and thanks to their clearly visible line, the French aviators were able, throughout the battle, to follow the advance of the infantry with accuracy.  The tanks attacked and cut off the villages of Méry and Belloy, enabling the infantry to capture the entire German garrisons without striking a blow.  On the 12th they reformed, and went forward again with the infantry, advancing east of Méry and Genlis Wood, before Belloy, and as far as the outskirts of St. Maur.  The line was advanced 2 kms., east of Méry, as a consequence of this thrust, and German counter-attacks failed to win back the lost ground.

RUINS
OF
BELLOY
CHURCH.

Cuvilly remained in the possession of the enemy, who consolidated it. On August 10, when the offensive by Humbert's Army began, the German line of support known as the "Vandalenstellung", which passed south of the village, was carried by the French in a single rush.

*The road leads to* **Belloy**, *which pass through, leaving the pond on the left. Just outside the village, there is a* "Calvary", *whilst a little further on, are* battery positions with shelters. **Méry**, whose church is in *the third street on the left, is next reached.*

The oldest parts of the church (choir, left transept and tower) date from the 16th century. The rest is 18th century. There are underground shelters in the village and surroundings, the entrances to which are nearly all blocked up. As in the other villages on this plateau, ancient *sarcophagi* have been discovered at Méry.

*Turn back and take G. C. 146 to* Ressons-sur-Matz. Trenches with wire entanglements are to be seen along the road.

ARTILLERY PASSING THROUGH RESSONS-SUR-MATZ.

## From Belloy Plateau to Compiègne,

### via Ressons-sur-Matz, Marquéglise, Margny-sur-Matz, Elincourt-St. Marguerite, Marest-sur-Matz, Coudun and Bienville.

*At the crossing of the road with N. 17, on the left, is* the CHATEAU OF SÉCHELLES. *Continue along G. C. 146; 2 kms. further on, there is a very bad level-crossing over a narrow-gauge railway. After crossing a normal gauge railway (l. c.) and another narrow-gauge line,* **Ressons-sur-Matz** *is reached. Turn left to reach the church.*

Ressons is a very ancient market-town. St. Amand, bishop of Maestricht, preached the Gospel there about the year 632. It was formerly a fairly important place, especially in the 16th century. A fortified castle, standing at the end of the village on the road to Séchelles, was taken by the Burgundians in 1430, and afterwards

RESSONS-SUR-MATZ. — THE MAIN STREET.

MARQUÉGLISE. — A CORNER OF THE VILLAGE.

recaptured by the French.   The church (*Hist. Mon.*) dates from various periods : the nave and side-aisle with their richly ornamented buttresses were rebuilt in the middle of the 16th century ;  the most ancient parts (cornices of the nave, and the northern transept and choir) are 12th century ; fragments of the stained-glass windows bear the date "1561". The building was considerably damaged in 1918 : the stained-glass windows were destroyed and the bell disappeared.

*Turn back, and beyond Place du Marché take G. C. 41 on the left. On leaving Ressons, there is a bad level-crossing over a narrow-gauge railway, another in very bad condition beyond Bayencourt Farm, and a third 1 km. further on, after which* **Marquéglise** *is reached. (See sketch-map, p. 114.)*

MARQUÉGLISE.
THE CHURCH AND FRENCH MILITARY GRAVES

The old Château opposite the church is in ruins ; the surrounding walls and outlying pavilions alone remain standing.

The church is mainly 16th century.  The choir vaulting contains several key-stones bearing coats-of-arms.  A pretty 15th or 16th century cross with a Virgin on one of its sides, which used to stand in the cemetery, was destroyed.

*A foot-path nearly opposite the church leads to* **Hill 77**. From there a fine panoramic view may be had of the battlefield on both sides of the Amiens-Compiègne road, as far as the Aronde, particularly to the south-west, where the view takes in Antheuil, Loges Farm (an old dependency of Ourscamps Abbey), and Porte Farm, formerly belonging to Elincourt-St.-Marguerite Priory.

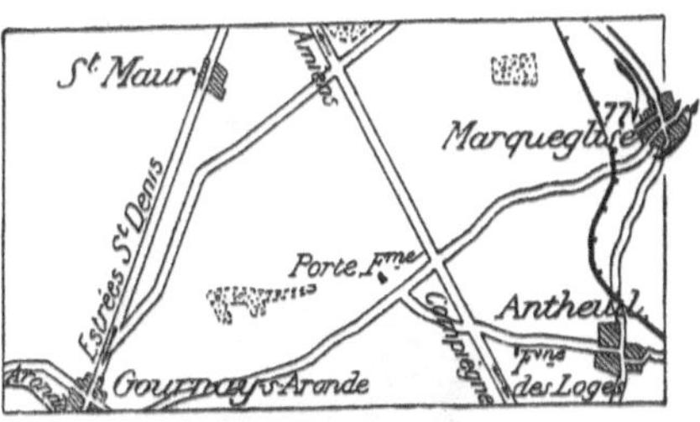



THE BATTLEFIELD
TO THE SOUTH-WEST OF HILL 77.

This region was the scene of desperate fighting during the German offensive of June 9-11, 1918.

On the night of the 10th, the Germans captured Antheuil and the two farms, advancing as far as the Aronde. They were already shouting victory, in the belief they were outflanking Compiègne from the north-west and would soon reach Estrées-St.-Denis, when the counter-attack of June 11 drove them back. Antheuil was retaken and held ; the two farms were likewise recaptured, but the French were unable to hold them.

On the 14th, although the enemy failed in front of Antheuil, they resumed their advance towards Les Loges and Porte Farm.

During the rest of the month this sector remained agitated. On several occasions the Germans attempted to retake Antheuil, but were each time repulsed.

A surprise attack by the French on July 9 resulted in the capture of the two farms in the early morning, with 500 prisoners. On the 13th, they improved their positions and advanced 500 yards to the north of Porte Farm. On August 10, the whole district was cleared by the advance of Humbert's Army.

*Return to the car and after turning it round, take the first road on the left to* **Margny-sur-Matz**. (*See map, p.* 124.)

The door and choir of the church are Norman. Some of the capitals in the choir (those behind the altar) attest to the primitive Norman style. A stone *Pieta* and a small ovoid stoup dating from 1603 have disappeared. A " glory beam " depicts Jesus-Christ, the Virgin and St. John.

MARGNY-SUR-MATZ. — INTERIOR OF THE CHURCH.
*Note the " Glory Beam ".*

*Continue along the road. On leaving Margny, there is a bad level-crossing over a narrow-gauge railway. Take the first road on the left to* **Elincourt-St.-Marguerite.**

This is a very old village, in the neighbourhood of which are several tombs dating from a very remote period. The country was occcupied by the Romans. Gallo-Roman remains have been discovered around the Château of Bellinglise. Under Charles-le-Simple, the village and chapel of St. Marguerite were given to the Abbey of St. Corneille at Compiègne. The Priory of St. Marguerite, founded by the Benedictines at the end of the 11th or beginning of the 12th century, was rebuilt in the 13th century. The district hereabouts suffered severely during the Hundred Years War. According to a local tradition, the old Château of Beauvoir, on the left of the Thiescourt road and now entirely overrun with vegetation, gave shelter one night to Joan of Arc, then a prisoner. This is not improbable, but the tablet in the church, bearing the following inscription: *Joan of Arc, before shutting herself up in Compiègne, in MCCCCXXX, made a pilgrimage to St. Marguerite and communicated in the church of Elincourt,* is not borne out by history, as she could not have gone to Elincourt — occupied by the English — seeing that she left Crépy to go to Compiègne.

Parts of the church are early 12th century, the aisles and belfry 18th. The doorway includes three accoladed windows, with two other windows above surmounted by diamond-pointed moulding. In the interior, there is an 18th century marble altar. A marble statue of St. Marguerite was placed in safety during the war, but another of St. John (15th century) also in marble, has disappeared, together with the two shrines of St. Barbe and St. Marguerite.

The church was seriously damaged, most of the vaulting being destroyed. At the eastern termination, the partial collapse of two buttresses laid bare some small 12th century columns which formerly ornamented the choir and which were walled in at the time the buttresses were reconstructed, probably in the 15th century.

*Leaving the church on the left, follow the road as far as the first crossing. Leave the car and climb the hill-side on foot, as far as the* **Monastery of St. Marguerite,** which dominates the whole valley of the Matz, and from which there is a fine view extending from Ressons Wood to the Soissonnais hills. Only fragments of the surrounding walls, a deep well, some cellars (which were transformed into shelters), and a number of old yew-trees remain.

ELINCOURT-ST.-MARGUERITE AND THE VALLEY OF THE MATZ,
SEEN FROM THE MONASTERY OF ST. MARGUERITE.

*On the way back, take the left-hand road, which joins G. C. 142. At the fork, take the right-hand road to* **Marfontaine Manor** *—* practically intact — built in the 13th century on a Gallo-Roman mound, to the north of the Priory Garden. The great hall has low vaulting, the central springing of which rests on a round pillar; the keystones represent three entwined fishes. The **Château of Bellinglise,** abutting on Marfontaine Manor, was built in the 16th century.

*The left-hand road passes near* **St. Claude Farm,** *at the crossing of G. C. 142 (from Elincourt to Lassigny) with G. C. 82 (from Mareuil to Thiescourt.* From here, there is a fine view over the battlefield from the Matz to the Oise : Gury (*to the north*), the valley of the Matz and Ressons (*to the west*), Mareuil-la-Motte, Marquéglise and Vignemont (*to the south*), Élincourt, Chevincourt, Mélicocq and Ribécourt (*to the south-east*), and the Thiescourt Woods (*to the east*).

BELLINGLISE
CHATEAU.

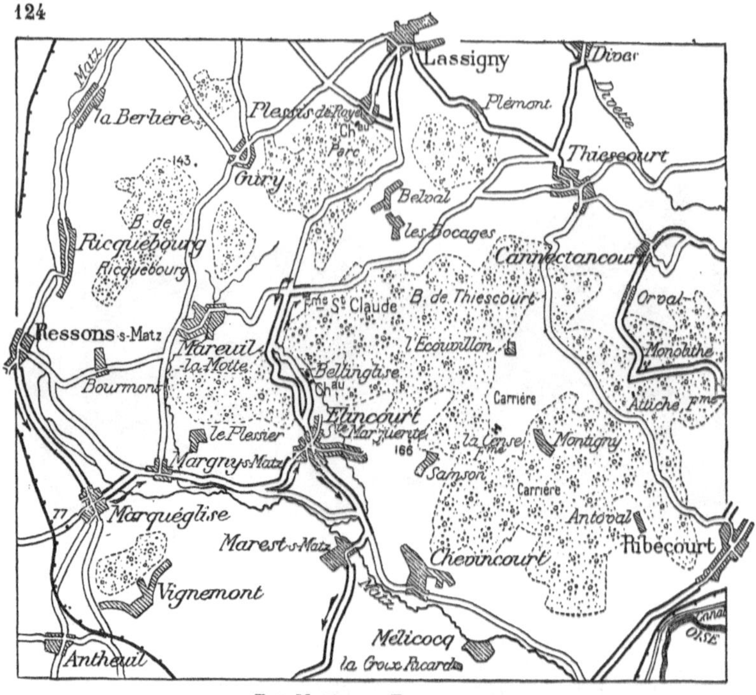


THE MASSIF OF THIESCOURT.

*The eastern portion of the massif and the fighting which took place there, are described in the Michelin Guide: Noyon, Roye, Lassigny.*

During the battle of March 30, 1918, the headquarters of General d'Ambly (77th Division) were at Élincourt, while those of General Guillemin (53rd Division) were at Chevincourt. At that time, these divisions were barring the road from Plessis-de-Roye to the Oise. Until June 9, the enemy attempted local operations only. On June 9, they attacked in massed formation, capturing Gury Heights, Ricquebourg Wood, and Mareuil-la-Motte. The village of Ressons-sur-Matz, in which they gained a footing, was disputed foot by foot. St. Claude Farm, which also fell, was in the thick of the battle. It was an important position overlooking the plateau, from which the enemy, from the outset of the attack, had an extensive view over a large part of the French rear positions, and its loss meant the withdrawal of the artillery. The brunt of the German attack was directed against this observation-post, which had to be abandoned, the French being overwhelmed. On the 10th the Germans reached Ressons Wood and Bellinglise Plateau, gained a footing in Marquéglise, and captured the farms of Attiche, Monolithe, Ribécourt and Antoval. On the 12th, after repeated attempts, they gained a footing in Mélicocq, carried the heights of Croix-Ricard, and crossed the Matz. However, on June 13, a French counter-attack drove them back across the river; Mélicocq and Croix-Ricard were recaptured, together with a hundred prisoners and a number of guns. In spite of several violent counter-attacks, the enemy were held.

On August 10, an offensive by Humbert's Army began to clear the whole region. At 4.20 a. m., the 129th, 165th, 6th, 121st, 74th,

ST. CLAUDE FARM.

123rd, 67th, 38th and 15th Divs. attacked from Courcelles to Antheuil and from Antheuil to the Oise. At 7 a. m. the first objectives were reached. Ressons, through which ran the enemy's main line (the " Gothenstellung ") was passed, whilst Marquéglise, the Château of Séchelles, Chevincourt and Bourmont were captured. The whole of a Regimental Staff was captured at the Château of Séchelles. At Ressons the tanks threw the Germans into confusion. On the 11th, Vignemont, Margny, Le Plessier, Hill 179, Mareuil-la-Motte, Bellinglise Château and Élincourt were captured. The French advanced in the direction of Gury and St. Claude Farm, which formed the key of the " Gothenstellung " position, and by evening had reached the western outskirts of Gury, a point south of La Berlière and Hill 143, and approached St. Claude Farm, Hill 166, Samson, Cense Farm and the quarries of Montigny and Antoval. On the 12th, they captured and progressed beyond Gury and St. Claude Farm, and took Écouvillon and Loges Wood, the latter being, however, lost again in the afternoon. On the 13th, they advanced along the plateau, gained a footing in Plessis Park, reached the eastern outskirts of Belval, and attained a point 800 yards north-east of Gury. Entering Ribécourt on the 14th, they re-occupied the Attiche and Monolithe Farms on the 15th, as well as the quarries situated 2 kms. north-west of Ribécourt. On the 17th, the Germans delivered several powerful attacks near Monolithe and Attiche Farms, but failed to drive back the French, who strongly held the newly conquered ground.

*From St. Claude Farm, return to Elincourt. Near the church, take Rue de l'Escalier (G. C. 142) and the road on the left of the Calvary. 1 km. further on, near a block of houses, follow the right-hand road, passing through* **Marest-sur-Matz.** *The road skirts the* CHATEAU OF RIM-BERLIEU, *opposite which is* a tower — all that remains of an old fortified castle. **Villers-sur-Coudun** *is next reached*, whose church is situated on the left, near the end of the village. The end of the chancel is 12th-13th century, the façade and vaulting 15th-16th century, the remainder modern.

*Continue along the road to* **Coudun,** formerly the Head-Quarters of the Training Camp built in 1698 for the Duke of Burgundy, grandson of Louis XIV. The king, accompanied by James II of England, paid a visit to this camp in August, to attend the military manœuvres. The camp, under the command of Marshal de Boufflers, extended along

VILLERS-SUR-COUDUN. — THE MAIN STREET.

the plateau which dominates the right bank of the Oise from Lachelle to Margny and from Baugy to the Château of Bienville. 50 battalions of Infantry, 52 squadrons of Cavalry and 40 guns were stationed there.

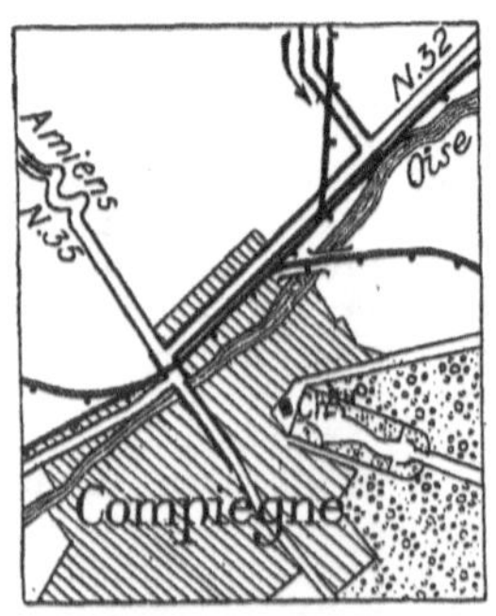


Although the nave and aisles of ST. HILAIRE CHURCH are modern, the façade, arched doorway and choir date from the Norman period (11th or 12th century). The doorway is ornamented with an archivolt formed by raftered and counter-raftered *tori* with a tympanum of diamond-moulding. One of the cornices of the choir is supported by Norman arcading with figured modillions. Inside the church are a stoup and a 7-branched chandelier (both made out of a single piece of wrought-iron), and a 17th century painting above the high altar depicting : *The Crowning of the Virgin.* The bronze bell (761) was saved.

*Keep along G. C.* 142 to **Bienville,** situated to the west of a long hill — the Ganelon — which stretches from the south-east to the north-west, and whose south-western side is sharply indented. From the top of this hill (altitude : 480 feet) consisting of a plateau which dips slightly down towards the Oise, there is a fine view over the whole of the surrounding country: Laigue Forest, Aisne Valley, Compiègne Forest, Oise Valley as far as Verberie, and the hills of Liancourt, between Creil and Clermont. At the north-western end of Ganelon Hill, many Roman medals and antiquities have been discovered, and it is believed that a Roman camp formerly occupied this site. Tradition has it that a fortified castle stood there in the Middle-Ages.

*C. G.* 142 *first skirts, then crosses the railway (l. c.), afterwards joining N.* 32, *at which point turn to right.* **Compiègne** *is entered by the Avenue de Clairoix and Rue de Noyon. At the end of the latter, take Rue d'Amiens on the left, cross the Oise, and follow Rue de Solférino which leads to Place de l'Hôtel-de-Ville.*

THE FRENCH G. H. Q. AT COMPIÈGNE, IN 1917.
GENERAL PÉTAIN MAKING HIS REPORT IN A ROOM OF THE CHATEAU.

*To visit Compiègne, use the Michelin Guide :*
Compiègne, before and during the War.

COMPIÈGNE. — FIRE AT THE CORNER OF RUE DES TROIS-BARBEAUX
AND PLACE DU MARCHÉ AUX HERBES.

*Extracted from the Michelin Guide :* Compiègne before and during the War.

# ALPHABETICAL INDEX

of the places mentioned in this Guide.

GERMAN TANK CAPTURED NEAR VILLERS-BRETONNEUX IN 1918.

XXIII bis-2.133-10-2015

IMP. KAPP, PARIS

www.ingramcontent.com/pod-product-compliance
Lightning Source LLC
Chambersburg PA
CBHW031302060726

47590CB00003B/1026